Ethics and the Professional Accounting Firm

A Literature Review

By

Aileen Pierce
University College Dublin

Published by

The Institute of Chartered Accountants of Scotland
CA House, 21 Haymarket Yards
Edinburgh EH12 5BH

First Published 2007
The Institute of Chartered Accountants of Scotland

ISBN 1 904574-24-6
EAN 9781904574246

Printed and bound in Great Britain
by T J International

Contents

Regard your good name as the richest jewel you can possibly be possessed of – for credit is like fire; when once you have kindled it you may easily preserve it, but if you once extinguish it, you will find it an arduous task to rekindle it again. The way to gain a good reputation is to endeavour to be what you desire to appear.

Socrates.

Foreword

In October 2004 the Research Committee of ICAS published *Taking Ethics to Heart*, an investigation into the ethical standing of accountants. It examined a number of remedies to ensure that appropriate mechanisms were in place to ensure 'good' decision-making.

This literature review is the third in a series of three commissioned literature reviews associated with *Taking Ethics to Heart*. This review is published at a time when the ethical standing of professional accounting firms in the eyes of the general public continues to be an issue for the profession and the corporate world at large and when regulatory and professional bodies seek to restore trust and confidence in the integrity of auditors.

The report identifies the issues which have been raised in the academic, professional and business literatures in relation to *Ethics and the Professional Accounting Firm*.

Chapter one explores the literature on professions and professionalism in general, and on professional accounting firms. The chapter aims to obtain insights into the evolution and ethos inherent in contemporary professional firms. The literature suggests that modern commercial and entrepreneurial ethos within professional firms contradicts and exerts pressures on traditional 'professional' values.

The next chapter reviews the literature on professional ethics and the objectives and role of ethical codes in accountancy. The literature emphasises that the consequences of accounting firms losing public trust are substantial and that accounting practitioners walk a narrow ethical line when responding to commercial opportunities.

Chapter three discusses the ethical dilemmas and challenges experienced by accounting firms; in particular the chapter concentrates on issues and aspects of accounting firm activities which have been criticised in the literature in the wake of the financial and accounting scandals of recent years. The chapter concludes that a redoubling of effort is essential to restore public confidence in the profession and accounting firms.

In the final chapter the report summarises the findings of the literature review. The literature suggests that the tensions created by professional accounting firms' pursuit of profit and growth targets can undermine traditional 'professional' values. The report concludes that a commitment from the profession to calling unethical activities and behaviour by accounting firms unethical and to imposing penalties that will act as deterrents is essential to promote ethical standards. The report recognises that the hallmark of a professional is the ability to exercise good judgement and that rationality and integrity must take precedence over rules to ensure good, ethical judgements prevail.

In addition the author identifies the need for further research to help inform and develop accounting firm and professional body strategies. This will require access to accounting firm personnel at all levels and to firms' policies and procedures. Questions which need to be addressed include: how does an accounting firm's culture develop?; what determines a 'good' and 'bad' accounting firm culture?; is zero-tolerence for unethical behaviour in accounting firms reasonable?; and can the focus on commercial success by professional firms be reconciled with high moral standards?

The Research Committee of The Institute of Chartered Accountants of Scotland, through the auspices of the Scottish Chartered Accountants Trust for Education, has been happy to sponsor this project and is pleased that the literature review is becoming available at a time when the subject matter is so topical and the profession's response is critical. The Committee recognises that the views expressed do not necessarily represent those of ICAS itself, but hopes that this project will contribute to the current debate on ethics and professionalism.

David Spence
Convener
Research Committee
December 2006

ACKNOWLEDGEMENTS

This report has benefited from helpful observations and comments from colleagues in the Accountancy Group within University College Dublin's School of Business, from Mary Canning and Bernard Pierce of Dublin City University, and from Christine Helliar, Director of Research at the Institute of Chartered Accountants of Scotland. Special thanks are due to Grace Collins for her research assistance at an earlier stage of the project and to Isobel Webber and Michelle Crickett for their patience, encouragement and professional support.

Executive Summary

Although accounting is a very valuable sort of knowledge, the notion that it might be a pure science that lacks weak sides and infirmities that need exposing is fundamentally improbable. It is also improbable that internal auditing of problems by professionals within the field will manage to fix every inadequacy, or that robust criticism from the outside can do damage to the real powers and virtues of economic quantification (Phiddian, 1996, p.77).

The Institutes of Accountants and their members have been subject to increasing public scrutiny following protracted criticisms in many jurisdictions over a substantial period. These criticisms are succinctly outlined in Lovell (1995, p.60) as:

...ranging from the failure of accounting documents to reveal a more accurate reflection of the financial well-being/ill health of organisations and the collusion of accountants in the preparation and validation of those documents, to the failure of the accountancy profession satisfactorily to take account of the public interest in the determination of the future of accounting and auditing practice.

High profile corporate collapses and fraud, with which accountants have been associated as auditors, executives and directors, have prompted searching questions to be asked as to the integrity of the professional accountants involved (Clarke *et al.*, 2003). These collapses or systemic failures, as the broad range of financial scandals exposed in the early years of the 21st century have been labelled, have brought into sharp focus and over a more concentrated timescale, issues of long-standing debate (Brown, 2005; Young, 2005; Reinstein and McMillan, 2004; Dewing and Russell, 2003) including: audit and accounting regulation; auditor independence; earnings management; and audit and audit firm quality controls. Twenty years ago, Briloff (1986) alerted the profession to the 'crisis of credibility' being faced because society perceived accountants to have lost their commitment to public service, a criticism that Briloff had also made some fourteen years earlier (Briloff, 1972). The credibility of the profession is threatened when the ideals of integrity, independence, public service and ethical standards come under suspicion. Similar to many commentators, Karcher (1996) believes that the ideal of any profession is public service, with monetary rewards playing a minor role. Self-interest can thwart this ideal.

The financial scandals at the start of the 21st century, including the expeditious demise of one of the then Big Five global accountancy firms, have brought the question of professional ethics in the context of accountancy into focus. This is not surprising, given that regulators and the public

> *...assume that the underlying problems [of the recent financial reporting scandals] are corruption and criminality – unethical accountants falsifying numbers to protect equally unethical clients* (Bazerman *et al.*, 2002, p.97).

Ethics have been shown to have assumed an increased importance in organisations, which are now subject to scrutiny and criticism from the media, regulators, and public interest groups (Axline, 1990).

Accountants and their professionalism have been criticised in the past, and some of the profession's responses to this criticism have been criticised as being self-serving. For example, concerns expressed outside the profession were simply reconstituted by accounting institutions as a problem of misguided expectations (Young, 1997; Radcliffe *et al.,* 1994).

However, the scandals of the early 21st century provided evidence that the commercial interests of large firms of accountants had overwhelmed the allegiance to professional integrity (Boyd, 2004).

Similar to the medical and legal professions, society grants public accountants an exclusive right to perform certain activities and it expects something in return (Mautz, 1988). Professional practitioners are expected to act in the best interests of society when resolving issues that arise within the scope of their franchised practice. The core issue in the context of the accountancy profession is the statutory audit monopoly privilege enjoyed by public accounting practitioners and the accountability that is demanded by that privilege. This monopoly is defended by the profession on the grounds of the profession's superior qualities of independence, integrity, and of serving the public interest. The relationship of these characteristics to ethical behaviour is central to much of the criticisms levelled at the profession over the past 25 years.

The accountancy profession has claimed to be both moral and ethical throughout the 20th century (Francis, 1990), but this assertion has been questioned in a variety of strands of academic research. One of the difficulties of evaluating the veracity of these claims, and the validity of the counter claims, is that moral schema and codes of ethics have undergone changes over time. Moreover, many of the underlying concepts are intangible and incapable of direct measurement. Prior research on ethics and the profession of accountancy has come from a wide range of disciplines and has focused on a broad range of issues. This report reflects a representative, rather than an exhaustive, insight into some of the more relevant literature.

The strands of the literature reviewed for the current study include: historical; critical; sociological; business ethics; professional ethics; financial reporting and auditing; sociology of work and the professions; histories of the accounting profession and professional bodies; examinations of the relationship between institutions of accountancy and the State; explorations of the meaning and interrelationships between a profession's authority, its responsibility and its independence; and theories of accounting regulation. These have all contributed to the current body of literature relevant to the topic of 'ethics and professional accounting firms'.

The accountancy profession comprises individual accountants, firms of accountants and accountancy bodies. Members of professional accountancy bodies engage in a broad range of professional activities that are all classified as 'accounting/accountancy' work. This includes: the traditional external audit function; other professional firm services; such as tax and corporate finance advice; finance, accounting and treasury functions in industry and commerce; and general management roles including those of chief executive, chairman and member of boards of directors.

One of the difficulties encountered in completing this literature review is the confusion, and often inter-changeability, in the literature between 'the profession of accountancy', 'individual accountants' and 'accountancy firms'. Much of the literature examines aspects of the accountancy profession where the profession can be interpreted as: professional bodies – institutes or associations; individual members; a collection of members; firms of accountants; or some combination of these. Equally, some studies examining aspects of auditors' behaviour or the environment can be interpreted as dealing exclusively with individual auditors, dealing with the accounting profession in general, or alternatively, dealing with audit firms.

This report, initiated by the Research Committee of The Institute of Chartered Accountants of Scotland, focuses on *ethics and the professional accounting firm*. However, it is debatable where *ethics and the professional bodies* fits into this structure, and where *ethics and the accounting profession* fits in. Convincing arguments supporting the view that the formerly Big Five accounting firms have had an enormous direct and indirect influence on professional bodies of accountants is provided in Boyd (2004). Many commentators refer to 'regulatory capture' whereby it is asserted that those who ought to be regulated by the professional bodies, the US Securities and Exchange Commission (SEC) and other regulators, have themselves come to exercise substantial control over the regulators because of their economic and political power (Hendrickson, 1998). Moreover, given that both the accounting profession and most professional accountancy bodies are made up of individuals and firms, it is perhaps inevitable that the profession and professional bodies feature in this literature review and the allied report on *ethics and the individual professional accountant*. Attempts to separate issues related to the individual from issues related to the professional firm highlight the complex inter-relationships between attitudinal characteristics of the individual *professional*, structural characteristics of a *profession* and confounding environmental variables, such as social, political, and economical.

The work undertaken to complete this literature review on 'ethics' and the 'professional [accounting] firm' has generated a substantial volume of material. However, many of the activities currently being highlighted by regulators and the media as manifestations of unethical behaviour by auditors, accountants and audit firms are not traditionally researched within an ethical framework. For example, there is a substantial body of research examining earnings management and/or creative accounting practices, as well as the impact of non-audit services (NAS) in compromising auditor independence. It is only in the very recent past that the link between ethics and earnings management and impaired independence has been explicitly highlighted in much of this literature. Prior to that, the focus was more on capital market effects generally, such as share price movements, as distinct from the integrity of information provided to that market. These areas of literature are major research topics in their own right, but very little of this published research features in the voluminous references identified by focusing on 'ethics' and the 'professional [accounting] firm'. A noticeable increase in relevant accounting-firm and ethics-focused literature has, however, been published since late 2003.

This report consists of four chapters. Chapter one deals with the literature on professions and professionalism in general, and on professional accounting firms. In order to coherently interpret the literature in relation to 'Ethics' and 'Accounting Firms', it is essential first to establish the history, nature and characteristics of professions in general, and the accountancy profession including firms of accountants, in particular. This chapter focuses on professional firms with the objective of gaining insights into the evolution of, and ethos inherent in contemporary accounting firms. In addition, key issues such as the meaning and context of the concept of 'public interest', the importance of trust in the profession and how these characteristics of the profession have evolved over time, are dealt with in this chapter.

Following an understanding of accounting firms gleaned from the literature outlined in chapter one, chapter two reviews the literature on professional ethics and the objectives and role of ethical codes in accountancy. Chapter three draws on auditing, financial reporting and the management control literatures focusing on ethical dilemmas and challenges facing accounting firms. Finally, chapter four summarises and concludes the report.

'Professions', 'Ethics' and 'Accountancy Profession' are all very broad themes. In order to operationalise the topic of 'Ethics and the Professional Accounting Firm', and to relate ethics and the professional accounting firm in this literature review, two research objectives are identified as follows:

(i) To establish the standard of behaviour that should be legitimately expected of accounting firms arising from accountancy's claims to professional status, from the commonly accepted link between professionalism and ethical behaviour, from accounting firms' fiduciary duties, and from the benefits derived by accounting firms from State recognition of their professional expertise; and

(ii) To establish if accounting firms in the context of moral or ethical benchmarks, have lived up to, or fallen short of legitimate expectations of their behaviour.

The literature reviewed in chapters one and two suggests that the accountancy profession has developed and grown over a protracted period with a reputation for integrity, independence and the exercise of expertise in the public interest. Given the privilege of State-granted monopoly over external audit services for public companies, the literature is also clear in its expectations of audit firms, that they should carry out their fiduciary responsibilities ethically, with honesty, independence, objectivity and without bias.

The second research objective is primarily addressed in chapter three under the overarching title of 'Ethical dilemmas and challenges', where environmental pressures and ethical challenges for accounting firms in their sphere of operations are discussed. However, because of the difficulty of directly witnessing ethical or unethical behaviour, a detailed examination of the types of behaviour which potentially support or contradict claims to ethicality is undertaken in chapters one and two, prior to examining the financial reporting, auditing, and management control literatures which offer explanations for the perceived trend of diminishing ethical standards within the profession in general, and within accounting firms in particular. Consequently, chapters one and two also provide insights into how accounting firms have fallen short of some of the expectations identified, such as by prioritising self-interest over the public interest, and by cynically using ethical codes to legitimise some activities including expanding the scope of services provided for audit clients.

Evidence of the expectations of accounting firms and their behaviour is taken from historical accounts, critical literature and empirical research. The empirical research presents mixed results on, for example, whether or not independence is impaired by non-audit services being provided by auditing firms or whether or not earnings management is ethical. This research often relies on proxies for phenomena that cannot be measured directly and is therefore subject to limitations. Moreover, the secretiveness of accounting firms is highlighted as a problem for researchers wishing to probe organisational issues associated with professional practice (Sikka, 2004). Some support for this secretive assertion can be taken from the recommendations relating to improved transparency of audit firms of the Co-ordinating Group on Audit and Accountancy Issues (CGAA, 2003) established by the UK government in response to concerns about the impact of financial scandals on the UK economy and capital markets (see Dewing and Russell, 2003 for a concise discussion of the recommendations). However, Gendron (2002; 2001; and 2000); Pierce and Sweeney (2005; 2004; and 2003); and Sweeney and Pierce (2004) have added to a growing number of studies successfully probing into the organisational functioning of audit firms in recent years. In addition, Bédard and Gendron (2004) provide useful insights to assist academic researchers wishing to take up the frequently articulated challenge to engage in more contextual, qualitative research to learn more about auditing practices, the audit environment and accounting ethics.

Chapter three discusses the pressures affecting the ideals of professionalism in accountancy in general, and accounting firms in particular. The main culprit cited in the literature is the prioritisation by accounting firms of the commercial ethos over professionalism and the consequent pressures, opportunities, and questionable responses, by 'Big Firms' in particular, to those opportunities and pressures. The question of whether it is right or wrong in a moral or ethical sense to prioritise commercialism and the corporate culture over professionalism and public-interest service is rarely directly addressed in the literature. However, the conflict between these 'business' models underlies most investigations into auditor independence and audit quality, and some research into earnings management and earnings quality.

This report is the third in the series of professional ethics-related literature reviews commissioned by the Research Committee of the Institute of Chartered Accountants of Scotland (Lovell, 2005; McPhail, 2006). The reviews highlight the breadth and complexity of the issue of professional ethics in the context of accounting. The variety of research questions investigated and research paradigms adopted in the extant literature could suggest an exhausted stream of enquiry. However, the reality is quite the reverse. Substantive progress in understanding and explaining the ethical proclivities of individual professionals, their collective institutions and business structures remains to be achieved. The concluding chapter of this report suggests some future directions prompted by gaps in the current research as it relates to the broad theme of 'Ethics and the Professional Accounting Firm'.

Chapter One

Professions, Professionalism and Professional Firms

The charges of all professional groups are onerous and subsist in the responsible and self-directed application of specialised expertise to matters of significance in the conduct of human affairs. … … Professions are relied upon to mediate … pressures in a manner that protects and enhances the public interest. Qualification to undertake this role must come from an occupational group's specialist expertise and demonstrated commitment to apply it responsibly (West, 2003, p.193).

Introduction

The process of professionalisation of a particular vocation or occupation is a complex and difficult project in which 'specific strategies sometimes fail'. However, 'once it is achieved it tends to deliver an enduring status' (West, 1996, p.91). Professional recognition is typically earned and maintained by occupational groups by reference to certain characteristics, behaviour, incentives and constraints on members' activities. In the context of accountancy, it can be argued that the behaviour of member firms is potentially more visible than that of individual accountants from the point of view of the public perception of accountants and their reputation. In this chapter, the literature on the nature of professions, professionalism and professionalisation is briefly summarised to provide a background against which the professionalisation process of accountancy and accounting firms can be understood and contextualised. This is followed by an overview of the literature examining the history of, and culture within, accounting firms. Finally, the literature on the relationship between accountancy firms and the State is reviewed in the last section of this chapter.

Professions and professionalism

In this section, theories of professions and professionalism are briefly outlined. In addition, the influence of structural characteristics of a profession, and the pervasiveness of the public interest in discourse about professions and accountancy firms is explored. Moreover, the importance of trust to professional status, and the charge that in recent decades, image has been emphasised at the expense of substance in how the accounting profession behaves, are explored.

A profession is described in Joplin (1914, cited in Preston *et al.*, 1995, p.518) as '[a]n occupation that properly involves a liberal education or its equivalent and mental rather than manual labor'. The liberal education anticipated was one that 'imbued the young person with such values as righteousness, wisdom and a sense of justice'. Nineteenth century concepts of professionalisation stressed the 'probity, dignity, honour and gentlemanly instincts of the practitioner' (Walker, 1996, p.12)[1]. More recently, a profession was loosely defined as an exclusive occupational group possessing a specialised skill based on esoteric knowledge (Abbott, 1983). The duality of a special kind of occupation and an avowal or promise was considered to be implicit in the notion of a profession (Mayper *et al.*, 2005; Neu, 1991; Briloff, 1986).

Early histories of the professions sought to examine the contribution made by professions to social and cultural life, and in that way, to explain their existence (Edwards, 2001). West (1996) provides an overview of the history of professions in general, and of the accountancy profession in particular. The classic model of the self-employed, autonomous professional evident in medicine, law and accountancy, has never existed in some professions, such as teaching. But even in the long-standing, well-respected legal and medical professions, as in accountancy, that traditional model has been supplanted in modern times by salaried employment in corporate or state bureaucracies (Abbott, 1988), where the increasing economic dependence of many professionals has forced them to relinquish control over many of the social and moral aspects of their work (Shafer *et al.,* 2002).

Four different perspectives on professions are identified by West (1996). The conventional *trait* theories of professions attribute altruistic motives to vocational groups pursuing professionalisation. These theories suggest that a checklist of particular attributes can be applied in distinguishing professional and non-professional vocations.

The second perspective is the functionalist view which extends the unilateral view of the trait model (West, 1996). That is, in addition to the attributes that distinguish a profession, professional status delivers benefits to people with that status. Under this view, a profession is granted an exclusive franchise by society to use its specialised knowledge responsibly to resolve issues within its specialist sphere in return for a commitment by the profession to act in the best interests of society (West, 1996; Lee, 1991; Mautz, 1988). A traditional functionalist view of a profession typically portrays it as possessing some authority, community sanction, an ethical code and a specific culture (Greenwood, 1957, cited in Parker, 1994) with both economic and efficiency benefits to society from these arrangements (Mautz, 1988). In return, the profession receives 'privileges such as self-regulation, protection from competition by the unqualified, and high social status and remuneration' (West, 1996, p.81). Traditionally, sociological studies of the professions were dominated by this view (Bédard, 2001). Professions were seen as integrated communities whose members possessed and applied complex and highly sophisticated knowledge to 'deliver expert services, the quality of which cannot be judged by the client' (Abbott, 1983, p.863), thus making it difficult for third parties to control or supervise a profession's activities (Mills and Bettner, 1992).

The functionalist view of professions has been somewhat discredited in much of the more recent literature on the sociology of professions because it has failed to 'appreciate the dynamic, procedural nature of professionalism' (Allen, 1991, p.51). Willmott (1986) posed one of the earlier challenges to this uncritical notion of professionalism in the context of accountancy. His seminal paper drew attention to the social and political attributes of practices and standards.

The third perspective is the interactionist view of professions (West, 1996). Within this view, a profession is an institutionalised form of control (Bédard, 2001). It is an aspiring occupational monopoly that seeks to further its own economic self-interest (Chua, 1986), is contextual, contingent and conditional in that it cannot be abstracted from the occupational group under study (Allen, 1991).

Finally, since the 1970s, critical theorists have developed the self-interest rationales that are more subtly included in the interactionist models. Their research accommodates Marxist and Weberian philosophies, sharing a 'scepticism of the intrinsic functionality of 'professional' groups and highlight the social relations and processes that enable the production and reproduction of 'professions' and professional privilege' (Chua and Poullaos, 1998, p.156). In this context, professionalisation is seen as an on-going attempt to 'translate one order of scarce resources – special knowledge and skills – into another – social and economic rewards' (Larson, 1977, p.xvii; quoted in Citron, 2003, p.247). Larson sees professions as occupations that organise themselves to attain both market power and social status 'by a process of public legitimation' of their actions (Lee, 1991, p.200).

The term 'professional project' was referred to in Larson (1977) as 'market dominance by monopolising social and economic opportunities and closing off opportunities to outsiders'. It was also characterised in MacDonald (1995b, p.188) as involving 'the occupational quest ...

for a monopoly in the market for services based on their [members'] expertise, and for status in the social order'. Professional dominance was defined as 'the ability of a profession to secure and maintain control over its work in the economic, political, social and intellectual spheres' (Willis, 1983, cited in Allen, 1991, p.51).

Structural characteristics of a profession

Regardless of which underlying theory of professionals and professionalism is acknowledged, certain characteristics are identified in the literature as essential to, or demonstrated by, professionals, whether an individual or a firm (Tricker, 1999; West, 2003). These characteristics are styled 'structural characteristics of a profession' by McPhail (2006) and they interact with attitudinal characteristics of individual professionals to influence behaviour and priorities within professional practice.

Cottell and Perlin (1990, p.18, cited in Moriarity, 2000, p.427) identify the defining characteristics of a profession as '[t]he capacity to regulate itself, often with the sanction of the law for those who violate acceptable norms of behavior'. Armstrong (1985, p.133) refers to an historical assumption that:

> *...professions could be defined by the possession of certain traits, notably independent, ethical or technical standards of performance and collegiate control of these.*

Magill and Previts (1991) incorporate these two aspects in their three essential criteria for categorisation as a profession:

- professional education;
- system of self-regulation located in a code of professional conduct; and
- government review and/or licensure.

Lee (1991) expands these criteria into a list of defining characteristics, as follows:

- theoretical body of knowledge;
- social prestige through charter of incorporation;
- training, examination and licensing;
- independence from client;
- code of ethics;
- use of rituals, symbols and specialist language;
- legal monopoly; and
- power and authority to self-regulate.

'Specialised knowledge' as a distinguishing characteristic of professions arises frequently in the literature that focuses on the traditional theories: traits; functionalist; and interactionist (West, 1996). In the more critical literature, such knowledge and its protection have been identified as the source of professional power, often abused in a self-serving way. Power is identified as a characteristic of professional privilege along with wealth and status (Canning and O'Dwyer, 2001; Portwood & Fielding, 1981, cited in Parker 1994; and Mills and Bettner, 1992).

Power in this context encompasses:

- control of knowledge and skills – control over technical knowledge through the development of new standards;
- self-regulation of the profession (self-regulation of entry and behaviour through uniform professional examinations, State licensing and socialisation processes);
- authority of practitioners;
- control of client selection and service;

- political bargaining with the State, to protect self-interests;
- influence upon government policy formulation, interpretation and execution; and
- ideological and cultural influence upon the community (influences in establishing, maintaining and changing moral standards and choices of society).

A key feature of the literature is that of serving the public interest.

The Public interest

> *Fundamental to a profession is the obligation of its members to maintain the highest standards of ethical conduct. A sense of responsibility to society and to one's own profession should be acquired very early in the educational process and can begin with the nurturing of moral and ethical values* (AICPA, 1988, p.10, cited in Ponemon, 1993, p.186).

Accountants are conventionally seen as applying esoteric skills, knowledge and judgements to complex tasks in the pursuit of their own and the public's interest (Zeff, 1972, cited in Preston *et al.*, 1995). 'Serving the public' or 'protecting the public interest' harks back to the Victorian notion of the 'professional gentleman', and to the older professions of the church, law and medicine (Preston *et al.*, 1995). At the core of professionalism is the claim to subordinate or, at least moderate, self-interest in service of the public interest. Referring to literature from the 1980s and earlier, Clikeman *et al.* (2001b, p.630) define professional commitment as 'the relative strength of a person's identification with, and involvement in, his or her profession', ethical orientation as 'the approach a person takes to making an ethical judgement' and professionalism as 'the extent to which a person possesses attitudes such as a belief in public service and a sense of calling in the field'. Public service and morality were contemporary ideals in the first decades of the 20th century to which the accounting profession appealed for its legitimacy. Accountants have been described as 'gatekeepers of the public's trust in our institutions' in the context of their role of conveying credibility to financial statements (Fischer and Rosenzweig, 1995).

Although a precise and universally agreed definition of 'in the public interest' remains elusive (Baker, 2005; 2004), public interest was defined as relating to 'matters of public concern, not public curiosity' in paragraph 2.4 of the Ethical Guide for Members of the Institute of Chartered Accountants in Ireland (ICAI, 2003).

> *Public concern extends to the concerns of clients, government, financial institutions, employers, employees, investors, the business and financial community and others who rely upon the objectivity and integrity of the accounting profession to support the propriety and orderly functioning of commerce. This reliance imposes a public interest responsibility on the profession. For example, audit serves the interests of society as well as those of clients. Auditors help to ensure the integrity of the financial statements presented to financial institutions in support of loans and to shareholders for obtaining capital. The public confidence is rooted in the objectivity auditors bring to their work. Investors, creditors, employers and other sectors of the business community, as well as government and the public at large, rely on the soundness of reporting by the profession and its impact on the economic well-being of their community and country.*

Thus, public interest in the context of accounting has been described as protecting the economic interests of professional members' clients and of third parties who place reliance on the pronouncements and advice delivered by both the professional body and its members (Parker, 1994).

Those third parties may include present and prospective shareholders, borrowers and lenders, regulators and the general public. The corollary, private or self-interest, has been defined in the context of professional accountancy bodies as protecting the interests of the professional body and of its members (Parker, 1994). Those interests include the professional body's social status, political power, and influence over economic and business activity. In addition, the social standing of individual members and their revenue-generating capacity is part of the private interest.

Lee (1995) argues that accountants in both the UK and the US have used the public interest argument continuously since the foundation of the profession in both jurisdictions as a means of protecting their economic self-interest[2]. For example, accountants in Scotland in the mid-19th century used the public interest argument to support their application for a Royal Charter. The formalisation of the profession at that time was a response to the perceived economic threat of a proposed bankruptcy law allowing lawyers to undertake work then dominated by accountants. The agreement of professional bodies to accept 'public interest' objectives with their charters also enables the sponsoring ministry of state (and other interested parties, such as company directors and financial journalists) to exert pressures on these bodies to acknowledge and honour their, however vaguely defined, public responsibilities (Sikka *et al.*, 1989). More recently, in the context of setting accounting and auditing standards, Lee (1995, p.59) concluded:

> *What the histories of UK and US standard-setting suggest is a delicate process, managed by the professional accountancy bodies, of balancing economic self-interest against public interest.*

The role of the accountancy profession in capitalist societies has been more explicitly articulated in much of the literature following the accounting scandals of 2001 and 2002 (see for example, Briloff, 2004; McMillan, 2004). It has also been argued (in Cooper, 2001; Sikka, 2001b) that accounting regulatory institutions have assumed greater legitimacy for facilitating and supporting capital markets rather than state agencies, who themselves may need to support other social groups and institutions.

Prior research illustrates the difficulty of being a professional with an explicit covenant to serve the public interest in situations where there are considerable economic incentives to adhere to self-interest (Peace (2006); Puxty *et al.* (1997)). The covenant is defined by Peace (2006, p.781) as:

> *A relationship premised on the interactions of people entrusting and accepting entrustment. The covenant relationship is a binding, enduring relationship of mutual loyalty that aspires to the common good.*

Briloff (2004, p.787) explains that:

> *...[t]his covenant was undertaken between our profession and society for most compelling reasons – reasons which have been increasingly compelling with the passage of time and the corresponding expansion exponentially ... of our economic society and the complexity of our corporate enterprises. It is to assure the effective functioning of capitalism with its corporate complex as the catalyst, which demands an effective system of corporate governance and accountability – and it is to oversee such a process that the covenant was entered into by society with our profession.*

In a study of published disciplinary cases in Australia, Parker (1994) concludes that the economic self-interest of accountants dominates their duty to the public interest. Other studies, focusing on the response of the profession to issues of accounting and audit failure, conclude that the client interest supersedes the public interest leading to concerns that the profession fails to make the powerful accountable and remains, itself, unaccountable (Canning and O'Dwyer, 2001; 2003; Mitchell and Sikka, 1993; Briloff, 1990). It is necessary to acknowledge, however, that it is potentially easier to find evidence where public interest has not been paramount in actions, policies and procedures of the profession, rather than evidence of where it has been standard practice to put public interest before private self-interest.

Nonetheless, despite substantial criticism of some accountants, accountancy firms and professional bodies, Briloff (2004) calls on the profession to re-dedicate itself to the independent audit on behalf of all stakeholders, while DeFond and Francis (2005) highlight the importance of auditing in maintaining credible financial markets and in supporting effective corporate governance processes. They caution against responses to inevitable, and potentially beneficial, investigations into high-profile corporate collapses 'degenerating into politically-motivated witch hunts that have unhealthy side-effects.' A research agenda focusing on the relationship between the organisational structure of accounting practices and their ability to serve the public interest is outlined in Shafer *et al.*, (2002) following a discussion of the impact on professional values of the growing trend in late 1990s America towards multidisciplinary practices and corporate ownership of CPA practices (see also Lucci, 2003). DeFond and Francis (2005, p.9) provide a comprehensive research agenda focusing on post Sarbanes-Oxley reforms in an effort to counter-balance some of what they describe as 'accusations that have been levelled against the auditing profession … based on anecdotes or shallow simplifications.'

Nonethless, society's trust that auditors perform their professional responsibilities in the public interest has been shaken by financial scandals. The role of trust is examined next.

Trust and impression management

Trustworthy information is essential for the efficient functioning of capital markets (Brown, 2005; MacDonald *et al.*, 2002)[3]. The public has an interest in corporate reporting being as close to 'the truth' as is possible (Hayward, 2003). Jones *et al.* (2000, p.30) define truth as:

> *The history of truth in accounting is most clearly played out in the evolution of the auditor's certificate. The auditor's certificate specifies the standards to which the auditor may be held responsible and, derivatively, the extent to which others should rely on the contents of the financial statements that have been audited.*

However, in an attempt to critically appraise the significance of recent financial scandals and to identify some different perspectives and perhaps some longer-term proposals for improvement, Young (2005, p.11) cited Phillips' (2001, p.8) caution that:

> *... truths [ie. answers] are slippery, elusive, tentative at best, always subject to new developments, new information, new alternatives ... Nothing is ever resolved once and for all.*

Nonetheless, in keeping with traditional values of the profession, Paterson (2004) exhorts it to focus on one rule above all others, to seek the truth, as reflected in the Scottish Institute's motto, Quaere verum.

Accounting and auditing play key roles in the institutions of business and State for ordinary citizens and investors (Brown, 2005). According to Gaa (2004, p.352), 'it is commonly believed that a primary value of the accounting profession is the trust that non-accountants afford them'.

Society trusts professionals 'to provide socially valuable knowledge in a competent and socially responsible way' (Neu, 1991, p.295). Explanations offered within the accounting profession for society's trust focus on its self-regulating nature. Explanations among academics focus on the disciplining nature of markets whereby auditors are assumed to have incentives to behave honestly and thus earn their reputation for integrity.

According to Bews and Rossouw (2002, p.377), the relationship between ethics and trust is 'ambiguous as ethics can promote trust, whilst trust can simultaneously be abused resulting in unethical behaviour'. The impact of the loss of trust on the accountancy profession in general, and on the auditing function in particular, is exemplified by the Enron/ Andersen story (McMillan, 2004). McMillan argues that the real value of Arthur Andersen was 'in the trade of conferring trust on company accounts through the implicit trust they held in the financial community' (p.944). The loss of trust magnified by the Enron debacle led to:

- Andersen disappearing from the commercial and professional landscape;
- 95,000 Andersen employees worldwide losing their jobs;
- partners in the firm losing most, if not all, of their investment in their firms; and
- thousands of Andersen people, who previously had reputations of integrity and honour, having those reputations tarnished.[4]

Traditionally, professionals were well-respected and trusted because they were assumed to have a coherent body of theoretical knowledge, altruistic motives, ethical codes, and arrangements for disciplining fellow professionals who abused their authority (Neu, 1991; Haskell, 1984). However, the concept of a profession has also been described as a social construct portraying an image that tries to project these socially desirable characteristics (Power, 2003; Neu, 1991).

Neu (1991) reviewed a substantial body of literature which suggested that the auditing profession had an interest in creating and sustaining 'a schema' that emphasised the trustworthiness of auditors. Impression management, though not labelled as such in earlier times, was practiced at least as far back in history as the 1930s in America when regulators responded to the 'moral crisis in capitalism generated by the 'immoral behaviour' of the capitalist elite' (Merino and Mayper, 2001, p.501). The securities legislation developed at that time was an attempt to 're-establish the viability of what was labelled the 'American Dream'.' Merino and Mayper argued that the first priority of that legislation was to establish the moral legitimacy of capitalism by restoring trust in the existing system. The regulation was perceived to be symbolic, a means of restoring investor confidence whilst preserving the status quo. It is argued in the literature that the moneyed interests at the time were not confronted.

Impressions can be managed in many ways. The following are examples identified in the literature where accountants were adjudged to be managing impressions:

- Accountants mould their professional interests and their clients' interests into the general social interest, and then present their actions as beneficial to society as a whole (Dezalay, 1997).
- A conventional strategy of 'doing nothing' when confronted with accusations of deficiency or impropriety - whereby issues are addressed seriously without altering the status quo (Humphrey *et al.*, 1992; Fogarty *et al.*, 1991; Briloff, 1990) - is also a political one involving adequate responses to concerns about accounting and auditing so that regulators are placated (Lee, 1994)[5].
- Words such as objectivity, professional judgment and ethics are used in times of financial crises such as bank failures, to reassure the public that self-regulation is working (Neu and T'aerien, 2000).

- The code of ethics, and discourse surrounding it, which are 'central to the spirit of the profession, are recast as part of a public relations campaign. .... [in] an overt attempt to fashion public perception' (Preston *et al.*, 1995, p.535).
- New accounting and auditing rules over time are introduced in response to threats of increased regulation. Some of these changes are sufficiently flexible to enable the status quo to remain while at the same time creating the appearance that the profession is taking action in response to criticisms (Byington and Sutton, 1991).
- The activities of the AICPA Special Committee on Standards of Professional Conduct (the Anderson Committee) and the Expectations Gap Standards of the AICPA Auditing Standards Board ... attempting 'to further the image of accountants as possessors of technical and esoteric qualities that are utilised in the public's best interests' (Hooks, 1991, p.110).

Neu (1991) undertook a study of Canadian Institute publications of the previous ten years, combined with interviewing senior members of the profession and 'ad hoc participant observation' over the previous three years to consider: (i) why trust was important to the public accounting profession; (ii) how the appearance of trust was created and sustained; and (iii) whether society at large should trust the public accounting profession. He analysed how the Canadian profession used impression management to convince its various publics that its claim to professional status was justified because of technical expertise (emphasis on education and training), moral or ethical behaviour and control over the body of knowledge. He argued that there were four sets of practices that helped create and maintain public trust: professional entrance requirements; maintenance of a professional technology, a handbook of accounting and auditing standards along with rules of professional conduct; good works activities; and disciplinary activities. These practices supported impression management activities of the profession aimed at maintaining and increasing its credibility and legitimacy. Taken together, educational standards for the profession and technical standards formed a set of constraints within which action occurred thereby limiting the possible range of behaviours available to accountants. However, flexibility existed which could facilitate bias to be exercised when there were competing interests. For example, auditors regularly made decisions that affected how resources were distributed in society. While the uninformed user, such as an employee or the general public, was invisible and difficult to empathise with, the informed users such as management and directors were generally immediate, and more likely than the uninformed user to be considered when a decision was being made. Neu (1991) argued that impression management practices resulted in a situation where:

- auditors were more likely to breach the trust of uninformed users when conflicts arose;
- uninformed users were unlikely to find out about these breaches; and
- uninformed users had no choice but to trust the public accounting profession.

By manipulating the symbols of integrity, expertise and service, the strategy of creating a positive image has been used by firms in the past to defend themselves against threats of external regulation. Baker (1977) analysed three strategies adopted by large firms towards a changing environment into: doing (delivering the service contracted for in an ideal way, with strategies for cost-cutting or revenue expansion); representing (activities a firm undertakes to improve its relationships with outside parties other than clients, such as a network of ties to lawyers, bankers and securities' underwriters); and being (creating a perceived need for the services of the firm on the part of the client, the business community and society in general). Other terms used to describe this phenomenon include impression management (Neu, 1991) and an ideological function (Humphrey and Moizer, 1991). 'Representing' includes overt marketing, publishing and community service. Baker (1993) argues that the publishing effort adds to the image of the firms' expertise and creates a societal and institutional presence and that the objective behind such representational activities is to position the large firms as an indispensable part of societal infrastructure. These findings were subsequently confirmed in an Australian context (Allen, 1991).

Mills and Bettner (1992) investigated the manner in which ritual was used by large public accounting firms to mask conflict arising from the perceptual gaps between the independent auditor's duty to society and the firms' need to satisfy clients. Sikka and Willmott (1995) argued that the accountancy profession attached considerable importance to its image of independence when seeking to defend and extend its jurisdiction. Using evidence provided by three case studies relating to events in the 1970s (corporate collapses), 1980s (harmonisation with EC Directives) and 1990s (criticism of accounting and audit regulation), they illustrated how the profession acted to defend and reinforce its image (p.547):

> *In its efforts to neutralise and discredit challenges to its aura of independence, the profession has developed and deployed a variety of tactics. These include revising its ethical guidelines, refining its disciplinary arrangements, as well as by mobilising other agencies, including the state, politicians, media, accounting academics, etc., in support of its claims.*

Following the unprecedented damage to the profession's image in recent years, the AICPA engaged in a marketing campaign in the US to emphasise the profession's competence and integrity as well as its intolerance for members who broke the rules (Abdolmohammadi et al., 2003). However, Abdolmohammadi *et al.* argue that in order to repair the damage to its reputation, the profession needs to focus on its selection of new entrants rather than on public relations and image. Research has shown that accounting students and auditors are generally unaware of the moral aspects of their discipline (Mayper *et al.*, 2005; McPhail and Gray, 1996; Shaub *et al.*, 1993). Abdolmohammadi *et al.* provide evidence that selection-socialisation in accounting causes a disproportionate number of individuals with the sensing/thinking cognitive style to be selected by the accounting profession. This cognitive style is associated with relatively low levels of ethical reasoning, regardless of gender. This evidence is consistent with Ponemon's (1992) conclusion that the selection-socialisation phenomenon may be operating whereby people with lower levels of ethical reasoning enter the profession. Mayper *et al.* (2005) suggest the problem is more fundamental. They find evidence that business education in general desensitises students to moral aspects of commercial activity and that accounting education, in particular, further limits students' ethical sensibilities and developmental capacities by its 'depiction of accounting as a mere technical discipline' (p.36).

Professional firms

The 'professional service firm' is defined as an organisation:

> *...involved in a variety of activities, from law, civil engineering and architecture to audit and accounting, consulting, advertising and software production'* (Morris and Empson, 1998, p.610).

The literature on professional accountancy firms consisted initially of historical accounts of formal practices being established in the style of legal and medical practices, which were the role models at the time when the earliest firms were set up. Subsequently, academic investigation focused on their economic and political success, their expanded influence throughout the 20th century, and more recently on their use and abuse of substantial power.

Historical context

> *Look behind the negative, green-eyeshaded stereotype – uncreative, introverted, pedantic, obsessed with accuracy to the last penny – and you have the positive image of a professional with the utmost integrity who never makes a statement, particularly one for third-party use, without having taken the greatest care to ensure that the statement is objective and appropriate. That's the image that has given our client a deep-rooted trust in the credibility and reliability of our services* (Luscombe, 1985 as cited in Neu, 1991, p.303).

Professional firms of accountants in Britain date from the late 18th century. Trade directories of that time reveal rising numbers of practising accountants in its major cities from around that date. Throughout the 19th century when accounting as a professional occupation became more formally established, accountants typically combined their professional practice with other occupations, such as banking, insurance, auctioneering and stock-broking (Kedslie, 1990). Accountancy in England and Wales was described as emerging from being an ill-defined commercial occupation into an established profession in the sixty-year period 1870–1930 (Kirkham and Loft, 1993).

Factors contributing to the success of early accountants included responding to a real need in mid-19th century British society, and explicit efforts to professionalise accounting activity. The rise of the profession was seen as a means of meeting the needs of an increasingly industrialised society (Edwards, 2001). The Joint Stock Companies Registration Act of 1844 in England formalised the separation of ownership and control in business organisations and provided for the proper keeping and audit of accounts. This created the need for independent professionals, with integrity, to vouch the truth and fairness of accounting information (Velayutham and Perera, 1993). The auditors' attest function developed within the social institutions of Victorian Britain and the importance of their social background is captured by McMillan (2004, p.949) in the following extract:

> *The tension the auditor had, between pleasing the client and providing the trustworthy attest function to shareholders and the financial community, could only be maintained through the professionalisation of auditors. Because these auditors were gentleman professionals, one could automatically assume they would have the moral backbone to resist any undue pressure from management. One would not be susceptible to collude with management because one was a gentleman.*[6]

Thus the external auditor's role facilitated accountants' arguments for privileges similar to those granted to doctors and lawyers (Velayutham and Perera, 1993). Early accountants attempted to emulate the characteristics of these 'older professions', such as possessing a theoretical body of knowledge based on rationalisation, a set of values based on the concept of 'calling' in public service, a code of ethics and the passing of rigorous examinations after a period of education and training (Velayutham and Perera, 1993). An early symbol of a knowledge base in the accounting profession was the introduction of professional journals such as *The Accountant* in 1874, *The Accountants' Magazine* in 1897 and *The Journal of Accountancy* in the US in 1905, together with professional body libraries. Other symbolic manifestations of professional respectability and social standing pursued in the early profession were substantial buildings, for example, to house the English Institute (Lee, 1995; MacDonald, 1989).

Social integration was also part of the professionalisation strategy of the emerging profession. Early accountants were educated, predominantly members of an elite grouping in their communities and they displayed social awareness by their association with members of the gentry and other professions, with the exclusion of women to elevate earning expectations, and by erecting barriers to entry (Staubus, 2004). Moreover, women were excluded for other reasons, which reflected other prejudices of the late 19th century, as highlighted by West (1996, p.88), who quotes from Roberts and Coutts (1992, p.388) as follows:

> *For an occupation like accountancy, which was involved in a complex struggle to achieve professional status, the risk implied by feminization was too large a one to take. ... [women] were not regarded as possessing the characteristics that make a good accountant; they were perceived as being too emotional and subjective, and not able to cope with figures.*

There is considerable evidence that early recruits to the Scottish profession came from middle to upper class backgrounds (Kedslie, 1990; Walker, 1988). Early Scottish accountants were associated with a range of different businesses such as canals, railways, banking, insurance, stockbroking and bankruptcy, depending on their geographic location and the strength of those businesses locally (Kedslie, 1990).

Concern with ethics and individual accountability was another part of the professionalisation strategy. This concern, noted by Preston *et al.* (1995, p.518):

> *...permitted and legitimised the claim that ethics was a 'state of mind' which was developed through proper upbringing and correct schooling. Moreover, this implied that it was not the profession's responsibility to provide moral training, but merely to limit membership to those who had already received it and continued to practice it.*

In a speech to the first general meeting of the then newly formed Institute of Accountants (forerunner to ICAEW), its first president explained the symbiotic linkage between ethical and moral standards and the prestige of public accountants, as follows:

> *...[S]omething beyond mere professional knowledge and capability must be brought into the field of professional action if the accountant is to maintain and consolidate the important position which of late years he has come to occupy in relation to the legal and mercantile community. By that something more I mean the qualities of unswerving rectitude – fearless independence – and single mindedness in the conduct of the business entrusted to him – such business being often of a very complicated and even delicate character – the due execution of which would be impossible in the absence of the moral qualities I have indicated* (Minutes of the Institute of Accountants, 1870-80, cited in Edwards, 2001, p.690).

Professional closure over time was achieved through a variety of mechanisms, such as expansion into certain areas of activity to near monopoly status, barriers to entry, legal battles with rival accountancy bodies and registration conferring rights to practice (Walker, 2004; Kedslie, 1990; Walker, 1988). Evidence of the rising public status of an occupational group is believed to be parliamentary recognition of its members' suitability to perform certain specialised tasks (Edwards, 2001). In addition, control over technical standards suggests control over the body of knowledge and thus professional monopoly of services. Protection of professional monopoly in the UK also relied on appeals to the notion that the public interest was best served by restricting the title of 'Chartered Accountant' (Lee, 1991). Having developed control over public practice, and established structures and networks similar to medicine and law, the structure of the accounting profession was stable until the early 1960s, as explained by Boyd (2004, p.378):

> *Most professional public accountants worked in public-practice accounting firms that provided tax and accounting services to*

> *businesses, other organisations, and to that small proportion of private individuals whose financial affairs were complex. The scope of most firms was local, with operations typically confined to one office servicing one town or city and its hinterland.*

UK emigration to the US prior to the First World War had a profound effect on both the development of institutionalised public accountancy at state and federal levels and on the founding and evolution of major firms in America (Lee, 1997; 2001). Qualified UK immigrants formed most of the predecessors of the US 'Big Five/Four' firms (Lee, 2001). Lee also provided evidence that the early development of these firms owed much to unqualified immigrant men without UK public accountancy qualifications. These unqualified men were more heavily involved than qualified men in establishing and managing the institutions of US public accountancy, possibly driven by their greater economic and social need to succeed in the US (Lee, 2001). Zeff (2003b) paints a picture of the American profession prior to 1940, building up its reputation and influence. Nonetheless, it has been suggested in the literature that accountants in the US are the 'provincial cousins' of lawyers and investment bankers (Dezaley, 1997), while in the UK/Irish capital market model, there is evidence to illustrate that the 'Big Six Firms are by no means economic pygmies' (Hanlon, 1997, p.845). The notion of a morally educated professional was also extremely important for the early US accountants. They were concerned with a culture of professionalism including integrity, character and personal responsibility (McMillan, 1999). By 1940, Zeff believes the profession had matured to the point where it embarked on a quarter of a century of being its peak in status and reputation.

Public accountancy in Canada is also similar to that in the US and the UK (Neu, 1991). Early Canadian legislation tended to mirror English legislation, whereas late 20th century legislation increasingly reflected the influence of American legislation (Murphy, 1986 as cited in Neu, 1991).[7]

The changing ethos

Accountants were historically perceived to be part of a solid, conservative profession with an impeccable reputation for ethical integrity (Boyd, 2004). Many early auditors were perceived to have come from the higher echelons of society (McMillan, 2004). However, Walker (1995) argued that early chartered accountants were not actually from the gentlemanly class at all, despite their appeal to this status. Nonetheless, they professionalised themselves by appealing to this professional ideal of educated, upper-class heredity, and by internalising it, and consequently raising the integrity of the group (McMillan, 2004).

Substantial changes in the profession from the mid-1960s have been documented, discussed and critiqued in the literature. Zeff (2003b, p.195) referred to the 1960s as a decade:

> *...when audit partners were, except in the rare instances of substandard performance, assured of tenure until they retired, and they knew that their firm would back them with its full resources when they stood up to their clients over questionable accounting practices.*

Accounting was described by Lee (1991, p.193) as 'one of the leading professions' in the context of the:

- number of people it employed;
- quantity and variety of services it offered and rendered;
- size and pervasiveness of its public firms;
- extent of its provision and use of educational and research resources;
- degree of influence it had in its relations with the State; and
- social status and economic rewards enjoyed by its members.

This description is remarkable for its absence of a quality criterion. The aspects suggested to contribute to the profession's standing are quantity and scope characteristics. Most of these have been subsequently identified in the literature as having contributed to the profession's diminished reputation and respect, witnessed at the start of the third millennium (see eg. Boyd, 2004; Wyatt, 2004; 2003). Strategic planning exercises conducted by the North American professional bodies in the mid-to-late 1990s revealed that both the Canadian Institute of Chartered Accountants (CICA) and AICPA had come to define themselves:

> *...in terms of the diverse breadth of activities undertaken by the Big Five rather than according to a core body of professional accounting knowledge' (Boyd, 2004, p.394).*

Hanlon (1994) suggested that the training of accountants towards the end of the 20th century had become primarily concerned with developing commercial awareness, being perceived as trustworthy and acceptable in a capitalist world, rather than exclusively developing technical expertise or serving 'public interest' values. Willmott and Sikka (1997, p.833), in a critique of Hanlon, paraphrased part of Hanlon's thesis in relation to the change in ethos that occurred over the 1980s within the accounting profession, as follows:

> *Uninhibited by the need even to pay lip-service to a public interest ethos, firms more openly promote ideals which encourage competitive individualism, with an emphasis on retaining clients, pleasing the customer (ie. capital) and promoting business virtues.*

Hanlon (1997) characterised the transformation of professional work during the 20th century as a move from 'social service' professionalism between the 1930s and 1970s to one of 'commercialised' professionalism since. He argued that the social service view emphasised the public good and technical ability, while commercialised professionalism required professionals to prioritise 'commercial issues, budget control, entrepreneurial skills' (p.843). He also described an erstwhile 'profession-state-capital compromise' under which certain protections were afforded to the profession in return for practising their expert skills in the public interest and carrying out certain of society's control and enforcement activities. This compromise had been replaced by increased demands for efficiency, accountability and service from professionals and increased exposure to 'scrutiny, market pressures and demands concerning the nature of services delivered' (p.844). Consequently, individual professionals began to change. Mautz (1988) distinguished between an 'EC' and a 'CPI' professional. The EC professional – 'expert competitor', was characterised as 'skilled, highly motivated, show-them-no-mercy-and-expect-none' role model who saw professional competitors as antagonists to be defeated, and not as colleagues sharing similar goals and philosophy. The CPI professional – concern-for-public-interest, had a different definition of success. These professionals had a degree of responsibility, wisdom and concern for public welfare (Duska, 2005; Mautz, 1988).

The modern firm

The accounting profession, as we currently know it, is comprised of individual professionally qualified accountants, accounting firms and professional bodies of accountants. However, systematic rigorous empirical research on accounting firms, their values and processes today is scarce due to their 'highly secretive nature' (Sikka, 2004, p.187).

Sikka and Willmott (1995, p.550) state that:

> *When we refer to 'the accountancy profession', we mean, first and foremost, those representatives of the major bodies and/or spokespersons of large accountancy firms who take it upon themselves to assert and defend the authority and independence of accountancy practices in general and the prevailing regulatory practices, in particular.*

Cooper (2001) argued that focusing research on large accounting firms in an attempt to learn more about professionalisation and its processes and consequences, and the preoccupation with issues of professional legitimacy in existing historical and sociology research, should be replaced by a recognition of the centrality of the profit motive for the accountancy profession. In a preface to a special edition of *Accounting, Organizations and Society* (1998) which illustrated a variety of 'quite diverse ways of exploring audit and consultancy in action', Hopwood (1998) identified a need to investigate the ways in which accountants' claims to professionalism were sustained, and the consequences of these measures. A number of studies over the last two decades refer to the limited available research on accounting or auditing firms (eg. Sikka, 2004; Zeff, 2003b; Cooper, 2001; Sikka *et al.* 1989). Sikka *et al.* (1989) refer to how little research up to that time had focused on evaluating the profession's delivery on its public service commitment. Zeff (2003b, p.189), when referring to his objective of examining:

> *(1) the challenges and crises that faced the accounting profession and the big accounting firms, especially beginning in the mid-1960s; and (2) how the value shifts inside the big firms combined with changes in the earnings pressures on their corporate clients to create a climate in which serious confrontations between auditors and clients were destined to occur.*

opined that:

> *...[t]he paucity of available evidence about actual changes occurring within the big firms, especially from the 1970s onwards, poses a major difficulty in conducting this kind of research.*

Difficulties of getting systematic data on accountancy firms' conflicts of interests have also been cited (Mitchell *et al.*, 1994). Cooper (2001) refers to how little is known about how professional bodies operate, who they see as their clients, and how they interact with other bodies, state agencies, corporate bodies, their own members and member firms. Sikka (2004) expresses similar reservations about the knowledge of value systems within accountancy firms citing the absence of research access to client data and live assignments as a particular constraint. Cooper and Sikka both believe that improved knowledge of these relationships would tell a great deal about contemporary professionalisation (see also Gendron, 2000). Most of the information available about audit firm organisational life comes from laboratory, questionnaire or interview-based research and from revelations from real or alleged audit failures (eg. from regulatory investigations into failures at BCCI, Maxwell, Waste Management, Enron, etc.).

Hopwood (1998) discussed the 'new audit firm' of the late 1990s. In its re-engineered form, Hopwood opined that audit firms prioritised business acumen over professional values. He also argued that rules, procedures, standardised processes and manuals characterised the activities of audit firms at the expense of discretion and judgement tailored to individual client circumstances (see also Hayward, 2003). Zeff (2003b) characterised the changing environment within major US accounting firms since the mid-1960s as one where 'admirable' features of the pre-1965 period were replaced. Table 1.1 provides a brief summary of how Zeff described the professional climate and how it changed from around the mid-1960s.

Table 1.1 Comparison of professional firm climate Pre- and Post-1965 (based on Zeff, 2003b)

Pre-1965	**Post-1965**
Vibrant discourse on matters of accounting principle among leading practitioners	Limited discourse for fear of offending major clients
Security of tenure for partners	Sanctions for not achieving revenue targets including dismissal
Firm support when standing up to clients	Firms siding with clients against standard setters
Partnership goal was career pinnacle	
Marketing campaigns for new clients unknown	Aggressive pursuit of new business
Rewards to partners were for quality of audit services	

The progressive concentration of the accountancy profession throughout the 1990s into six (which subsequently became five, then four) firms, whose clients were large international companies, reflected a general contradictory trend towards monopoly within capitalist economies where the virtues of competition were regularly extolled (Willmott and Sikka, 1997). Beattie *et al.* (2003) discuss the paradox of concerns within the profession in the early 1990s that the large accounting firms were competing too aggressively at the same time as extreme market concentration suggested concerns for potentially anti-competitive behaviour. Byington and Sutton (1991) argue that monopoly power in the hands of the self-regulated public accounting profession has produced welfare losses to consumers of audited financial statements, such as investors, creditors and the public at large. The dominant position of the large firms has also allowed them to influence the creation of GAAP and GAAS. In a critique of Hanlon's book on the commercialisation of accountancy (Hanlon, 1994), Willmott and Sikka (1997) argue that the big accountancy firms emerged 'as key players' in the restructuring of western business and public sector activities in response to the economic shocks to Western economies of the 1970s and 1980s, such as greater competition from more efficient low-cost economies in the Pacific Rim and the 1970s oil crisis. They describe the emergence of the major accountancy firms, as follows:

> ... *[T]hrough a relentless process of merger and concentration, the big accountancy firms have emerged as key players in the restructuring game, and, as architects, facilitators, and evaluators of efforts to restore competitiveness, accountants have been amongst its major beneficiaries* (Wilmott and Sikka, 1997, p.838).

The culture and 'tone at the top'

Andersen-Gough *et al.* (2001) describe socialisation as a complex accomplishment, involving induction into a wide array of formal and informal norms, both taught and learned, consciously and subconsciously. Fogarty (1992) defined it as 'the process by which individuals are moulded by the society to which they seek full membership'. A number of researchers have analysed the socialisation processes of accounting firms (eg.. Fogarty, 2002; Cohen *et al.*, 1993). The challenge of managing multicultural personnel in global firms to ensure consistency of standards and ethical judgements is examined in some of this research (Jeffrey *et al.*, 2004; Arnold *et al.*, 1999; Pratt *et al.*, 1993).

Hanlon (1994) explained that the socialisation and recruitment processes of the then Big Six firms changed over time to allow the firms to legitimise themselves in the eyes of their clients and to present what they did as professional in the more recent meaning of the word, ie. as commercially driven and entrepreneurial. He argued that these characteristics had come to be seen as values which fostered international competitiveness and, therefore, were deemed to be socially desirable (Hanlon, 1997).

Phiddian (1996, p.76) noted:

> *It is very easy to become naturalised to the conventions of an intellectual discipline, so that its language comes to feel natural and sufficient for all things; professional formation can also be professional deformation.*

Douglas *et al.* (2001) noted that, while the socialisation process was important in all professional firms, it was of particular importance in the accounting profession because neither employee behaviour nor output relative to performance were readily measurable. Therefore, in order to limit employee opportunism and inefficiencies that might be caused by incongruence between individual and organisational goals, the accounting profession had to rely on 'clan control' (Ouchi, 1979 and 1980). Clan control is the operation of strong common values to control opportunism and/or inefficiencies. Such values are manifested in organisational practices – the 'feel' or the 'climate', as understood by employees through their perceptions of the events, practices, procedures, and behaviours that are expected, rewarded, supported, or discouraged. A complimentary way of describing the socialisation process within the professions is what has been described as operating within 'a professional space' (Abbott, 1988). McMillan (2004, p.945) notes:

> *The space for the US profession includes among others the activity of the public accounting firms, the financial and auditing standards regimes, the professional and licensing bodies, the professional schools within the university system, as well as the outside forces such as the regulations of the stock exchange, the SEC and other governmental regulatory bodies, and the creators and users of financial accounting information within the increasingly global capitalistic structures.*

McMillan describes clan control in a slightly different way to Ouchi. He suggests that the professional space, like the one within which the accounting profession operates, can have two types of discipline, the discipline of enclosure and the discipline of space. Enclosure controls, in the case of accounting, are the rules which set the boundaries of who is allowed to be in the profession and who is not. The discipline of space is more subtle. It is directed at individuals, while simultaneously being very general. The discipline of space is enforced using supervisory, hierarchy, and reward systems. Within this discipline, the profession controls itself through expounding the various ideals of the profession, including the virtues and character needed to be a 'good accountant'. This discipline of space or, as Ouchi (1979) refers to it, 'clan control', exerts behavioural control while simultaneously creating the ideal of the individual prudent professional offering expert judgement within particular settings.

Social psychology generally predicts that organisational values and goals dominate those of individuals (Sims and Brinkman, 2003; Shafer *et al.*, 2002). A subset of organisational culture is the ethical culture created through management practices and espoused values. In essence, individuals' attitudes to ethics and the concept of ethical behaviour is heavily linked to the ethical 'environment' in which they operate (D'Aquila, 2001). Theories of ethical decision-making commonly acknowledge the influence of organisational value systems on individual decision-making and behaviour (Mayper *et al.*, 2005; Roberts and Dietrich, 1999; Hunt and Vitell, 1986). Mills and Bettner (1992) identified a role ambiguity gap in audit firms whereby conflict arose between the values and norms that the firms projected to their professional staff and the professional staff's perceptions of those values and norms. They argued that large firms used rituals to mask conflicts arising from these gaps. The literature highlights the need for sincere commitment over time from top management if an ethical environment is to endure (Bews and Rossouw, 2002).

Ideological desensitisation can become a defensive response to the loss of control over professional work experienced by employed professionals (Shafer *et al.*, 2002). By focusing primarily on advancing their technical knowledge and skills rather than on moral aspects of their work (Mayper *et al.*, 2005), these professionals avoid value conflicts. By adapting individuals' goals to those of their employers, many professionals can associate their professional identity with their technical expertise rather than with the ideals and values of practice. In the context of conflicting messages, a potentially prophetic warning was sounded by Phiddian (1996, p.77) when he referred to the role of language including corporate hype, management jargon and public service doublespeak in the collapse of the State Bank of South Australia in the late 1980s. As discussed in Meehan (1997), he stated:

> *A corporate culture that is obsessed with growth but speaks in the correct professional codes can blind itself to imminent ..... disaster.*

Young (2005) discusses how organisational imperatives, such as the need to find more profits, can galvanise hundreds of thousands of individuals to work towards a corporate goal with blindness to the broader implications of their actions. In the context of the recent corporate financial scandals, she described how the:

> *...creative work activities of these many individuals were typically directed toward the end of producing more – more profit, more revenues, and higher stock prices.*

The surrounding bureaucracy focused attention upon the tasks and effectively distanced people from the consequences of their actions. In an experiment examining whether social influence pressures within an accounting firm affected auditors' willingness to sign-off on financial statements that were materially misstated, Lord and DeZoort (2001) found that obedience pressure from superiors significantly affected willingness to sign-off prematurely, while conformity pressures from peers did not.

Because the organisational values of accounting firms are so important (Douglas *et al.*, 2001) and are heavily relied upon as a means of control (McMillan, 2004), the atmosphere in which employees carry out their responsibilities influences whether or not employees behave ethically. Senior management plays a key role in determining the corporate environment, and although the single most effective way for management to send a signal of the management tone is by leading by example, management must also communicate an expectation of high ethical standards (D'Aquila, 2001). Chonko and Hunt (1985) indicate that specific actions by top management to encourage (discourage) ethical (unethical) behaviour decreases the extent of ethical problems perceived by CPAs. Actions that managers can take to reduce ethical dilemmas faced by subordinates have been identified in the literature (Johnstone *et al.*, 2001; Finn *et al.*, 1988). First, they can act as role models and not send ambiguous/conflicting signals; second, they can discourage unethical behaviour; and third, they can develop, promote and enforce a code of conduct. Explicit training for auditors on how to deal with situations where client management exerts pressure on judgement-based decisions because financial incentives exist is recommended (Johnstone *et al.*, 2001). This should include negotiation skills and tactics, in addition to more typical training on how to comply with independence rules, such as those relating to share ownership.

A self-selection mechanism has also been identified in the context of accounting firms where firms hire and promote individuals who fit into the prevailing firm culture, and where individuals unable to fit in, leave. Research by Ponemon (1992) on ethical reasoning and its effects on the hiring and retention decisions of public accounting firms suggested that management of accounting firms hired and promoted only those individuals who shared a common set of ethical values and beliefs. His research set out:

> *...to explore the influence of accounting firm socialisation upon the individual CPA's level of ethical reasoning. ... Findings ... corroborate the existence of ethical socialisation whereby those progressing to manager and partner positions within the firm tend to possess lower and more homogeneous levels of ethical reasoning. Experimental findings also suggest that firm managers' promotion decisions are biased in favour of individuals possessing ethical reasoning that is closer to their own capacity. This implies that the ethical culture of the accounting firm stymies an individual's development to higher levels of ethical reasoning* (Ponemon, 1992, p.239).

Abdolmohammadi *et al.* (2003) reinforce Ponemon's findings and report that not only does selection-socialisation occur, but that the type of individual attracted ('sensing-thinking') is associated with relatively low levels of ethical reasoning. They concluded that this made it difficult to foster the 'ethical' climate in which accountants purported to operate. However, the consensus on selection-socialisation was contradicted in a longitudinal study of US CPAs randomly selected nationally in 1994-1995 and 2000-2001 (Scofield *et al.*, 2004). In analysing the conflicting results, Scofield *et al.* claimed superior rigour in their study and, therefore, disputed the generalisability of Ponemon's (1992) findings. In addition, by including a random sample of attorneys from all over the US in their 1995 sample, Scofield *et al.* provided further evidence that accountants demonstrated lower 'P' (moral development) scores than other professional groups (see also Armstrong, 1997; Ponemon and Glazer, 1990).

Self Regulation and the State

Baggott (1989) acknowledged that self-regulation tended to prevail where co-operation was essential for the implementation of government policies and where the regulated had a monopoly of technical expertise in a particularly important policy area. However, public pressure is often a factor in the reform of a self-regulatory system. Although public pressure usually calls for more State intervention, changes in the self-regulatory system tend to follow, thus illustrating the role of self-regulation as an instrument of compromise, balancing public and private interests.

Mautz (1988, p.122) notes that:

> *The essence of a profession in the traditional sense is found in the grant by society of a special franchise, in return for which the practitioners of that profession accept responsibilities to provide a degree of regulation and enforcement through expert advice and persuasion, thereby relieving society of the burden of providing that control by other means.*

Luehlfing (1995) proposed a theory of self-regulation in the context of the accounting profession which was grounded in the relationship between three institutions: the public; the political establishment; and the accounting establishment. He explained the interaction between these three in terms of crisis, public outcry, political response, accounting intervention and probation. The political establishment provided an alternative to legislation by allowing the accounting profession to self-regulate and placed the profession on 'probation' and assured the public that the accounting establishment would be closely monitored (Luehlfing, 1995). Luehlfing illustrated this theory using five historical events in the US covering the period 1907 to 1987 and by critically reviewing the drivers of the, then, current self-imposed accounting and auditing regulatory environment. This theory was supported, in the context of the UK chartered accountancy bodies, by Willmott *et al.* (1993, p.71) who argued:

> *The Charter also places its [any chartered association's] members in a strong position to be granted a monopoly (by the state) over certain areas of business ... and to be accorded responsibility as private interest governments, for public policy making in the area of setting and enforcing ... standards ... From the standpoint of politicians and their advisors, the economic appeal of self-regulation lies in the not-insignificant administrative savings derived from private sector regulation of accounting labour; and its political appeal lies in cushioning politicians ... from responsibility for any perceived failures of regulation ...*

Within the accountancy profession, large accountancy firms are influential across a broad range of societal activities: commerce; health; transport; diplomatic services; local government; defence and security; and education (Willmott and Sikka, 1997). Many of the critical researchers focus on the role of the State in supporting the economic well-being of professionals and in not challenging the deficiencies of certain elite groups (see eg. Mitchell *et al.*, 1994; Sikka and Willmott, 1995; Willmott and Sikka, 1997; Hanlon, 1997). Analysing the role of the State in supporting the status quo within the accounting profession, they have been critical of the State's reluctance to hold the profession accountable for audit failures, perpetuating the notion that such failures are consequences of 'some individual's incompetence rather than the control regimes operating within the firms' (Willmott and Sikka, 1997, p.840). Willmott and Sikka (1997, p.840) conclude that:

> *...such obfuscation has continued to promote confidence in the aura of accounting and accountants to portray an objective state of corporate financial affairs and fuel the demand for their services.*

As Willmott and Sikka see it, the State has facilitated an expansion of the jurisdiction of accountants and accountancy firms.

Hanlon (1997) asserts as an irrefutable fact that the State has benefited certain professional groups and limited the role of others. He used privatisations in the UK to illustrate his case, saying that such programmes benefited accountants, bankers, and corporate lawyers. The interplay between the State and the profession has been referred to as the 'game of self-regulation' within which auditors seek to maintain self-regulation and avoid real or imagined State interference, while simultaneously cultivating State backing to obtain and maintain the professional monopoly over prescribed audit services (Lee, 1994). Lee argues that 'auditors' achieve this generally by balancing their self interests with the interests of stakeholders and the State, and particularly, by managing the expectations gap. Lee (1994, p.32) argues that:

> *The balancing ... involves a two-edged sword – one edge providing potential benefit by assisting in the social construction of the audit profession via perceptions of the existence of a reputable body of knowledge; the other creating a mixture of possible disbenefit because of an enlarging of the expectations gap, and possible benefit as a result of successfully managing the enlargement.*

Sikka (2004) continues to argue that accounting firms are subject to very little accountability despite the importance to them of the State-granted monopoly for audit services. Until relatively recently in the UK, the State referred the outcome of its investigations into fraud, collapses and scandals to the professional bodies who were expected to take action against the implicated firms and members (Mitchell *et al.*, 1994). It has been suggested that the apparent reluctance of the State to intervene in the accountancy profession's disciplinary processes has been related to the its concern not to damage the perceived reputation and credibility of a profession that is central to confidence and trust in capital markets (Mitchell *et al.*, 1994). This 'indulgence and inaction inevitably supports and fuels an ethic of self-interest amongst accounting practitioners' (Mitchell *et al.*, 1994, p.49).

Summary

Accounting firms are made up of individual professionals and other principals and employees. They are part of the institutional structure of the accountancy profession as members of professional accountancy bodies. Membership of specific professional bodies attracts the privileged right to provide certain State-regulated services, and in return, assumes obligations. The literature argues that these obligations include the moral imperatives of independence, objectivity and integrity. Public expectations of accounting firms are based on the image created and nurtured by the firms, by professional body structures and processes, and by audit firms' public relations and advertising. This image is one of a noble profession providing services in the public interest, with self-interest secondary to protecting the interests of those who rely on the superior expertise and reputation for fairness and objectivity of practitioners. The literature reviewed in this chapter presents a somewhat critical view of the accountancy profession as it has developed over time. It casts doubts over whether or not accounting firms, possibly aided by professional bodies, sincerely practice what they purport to represent. It also suggests that the modern commercial and entrepreneurial ethos within professional firms contradicts and exerts dysfunctional pressures on traditional professional values.

Nonetheless, the profession holds on very tightly to the traditional positive image of accountants as reliable, independent experts of impeccable integrity. The integrity of practitioners is reflected in accounting firms' traditional claims to ethical behaviour and adherence to professional ethical codes. The literature on professional ethics and ethical codes is briefly reviewed in chapter three to provide insights into the role of this central cultural inheritance in the ethical profile of accounting firms.

ENDNOTES

1. See Bédard (2001) and Parker (1994) for further traits identified in prior research.
2. See also Willmott *et al.*, (1993) for a discussion of public interest and its meaning and for an insight into how professional bodies construct their mission, with respect to their claims to protect the public interest.
3. MacDonald *et al.* (2002) explain the benefits of a co-operative relationship founded on trust as including saving costs of 'monitoring, auditing, enforcing rules for every miniscule transaction.'
4. The phrase used by McMillan (2004) to describe the value of post-Enron reputations of Andersen employees ,'almost worthless', possibly overstates the effect as many former Andersen employees throughout the world transferred seamlessly to other major accountancy firms with relatively minor impact on their careers.
5. It also retains a sufficient expectations gap to maintain a zone of discretion for professional judgement and consequently, facilitates engineering a widening of the scope of audit.

6. It has been argued that with increasingly sophisticated technology available in the last quarter of the 20th century, the profession faced the risk of 'proletarianisation' which results when the work of the profession becomes increasingly routine, rationalised and codified (Allen, 1991).

7. See also Neu *et al.* (2003) for a comprehensive and insightful discussion of the importance of the character-based ethic to the profession using an analysis of practitioner-directed discourse in the Canadian profession's official magazine.

Chapter Two

Professional Ethics

Ethics is about an attitude of mind and the determination of actions according to a set of usually subjective and sometimes conflicting values (Bromell, 2004, p.131).

Introduction

The professions affect the interests and well-being of individuals who depend on professional services. For example, the accountancy profession affects how income is measured, what tax is paid, how wealth is distributed, resources are allocated, risk is assessed, capital markets operate, and how pensions are measured and managed. Professions exert influence on key social institutions that pursue the common good. Thus, society is entitled to evaluate professional performance in light of a moral as well as a technical code (Francis, 1990; Frankel, 1989). Chapter one examined the nature of professions and professionalism and argued that the ethos and culture of accounting firms had changed substantially over time. The main change identified is that of firms becoming more commercially focused and less concerned with their public interest obligations, contrary to the image generally portrayed by the profession of a noble and ethical activity. In this chapter, the meaning and relevance of professional ethics, ethical behaviour, ethical decision-making and ethical codes in the context of accountancy are explored through the relevant published research. This literature is reviewed to clarify the expectations of professional firms and to evaluate the significance of codes in the context of the professional firm environment. Legitimate expectations of firms are identified from the literature to operationalise the theme 'ethics and the professional firm'.

Meaning of professional ethics

Ethics refers to a discipline in which matters of right and wrong, good and evil, virtue and vice, are systematically examined (Brinkmann, 2002). The literature suggests that professional ethics serve a potentially contradictory dual role (Parker, 1994). They encourage a sense of social responsibility in the professional member (Tucker *et al.*, 1999), while simultaneously providing justification for professional self-interest (Fisher *et al.*, 2001).

Abbott (1983) analyses three theories of professional ethics but concludes that they are not mutually exclusive. The functionalist or, 'control of expertise' theory, suggests that professional ethics derives from the inherent social danger of uncontrolled expertise. This is close to Parker's (1994) public interest view of ethics. Within this concept of professional ethics, ethical codes and disciplinary enforcement by the profession are major components of control mechanisms devised to protect clients (Bédard, 2001). The second theory is the monopoly theory which perceives ethics to be more aggrandisement rather than control (Citron, 2003), while the third theory is described as 'high status' theory wherein ethics is viewed as determining extra- and intra-professional status.

Steiner (1972) defines ethical behaviour in organisations as conduct that is fair and just, above and beyond constitutional laws and applicable government regulations. Ahadiat and Mackie (1993, p.243) refer to there being 'no one clear definition of 'ethics' or 'ethical behaviour'. In the context of the public accounting profession, there is an assumption that 'accountants would act according to the rules promulgated by the profession as well as common ideals or goals regarding integrity, objectivity and competence' (Magill and Previts, 1991, p.8). Roberts and Dietrich (1999, p.989) argue that there is no unique professional ethic:

> *The professions are not unique is possessing an ethic. Rather, we prefer to view ethics on a continuum ranging from purely individualistic to purely socially constructed, which can be applied to all occupations. Decision-making in professions is placed closer to the socially constructed end of the spectrum whereas decision-making in non-professional business is closer to the purely individualistic end. There is no unique professional ethic; it is simply that professionals are involved in areas where the significant externalities involved in transactions warrant broader social constraints on behavior. The acceptance of these constraints is necessary in order to gain social recognition as a profession.*

Ethics and Accountancy

At one extreme, it can be argued that the role played by accountants and accountancy in facilitating capital accumulation is unethical (Willmott and Sikka, 1997). For example, accountancy firms offer advice on mergers and rationalisations, but they have no responsibility to workers who are subsequently made redundant, or whose psychological or physical health is damaged by cost-cutting measures. However, in the context of capitalism providing the benefits of employment and opportunities within society, the role of accountants and accountancy can be more positively perceived because they support and facilitate accountability, enterprise and good governance.

Much of the discussion of the nature and role of professional ethics in the context of accountancy is grounded in the North American profession. Neu and T'aerien (2000) argue that although early Canadian discourse around notions of professional ethics implied a connection between ethics and fair and honourable dealing, and a connection with 'honour, rectitude and objectivity', there was almost no discussion of these terms, nor of how they contributed to professional ethics. Preston *et al.* (1995) demonstrated that discourse surrounding the development of the first US code of ethics of 1917 and changes reflected in the later code developed in the 1980s reflected contemporary challenges to the legitimacy of accountants as well as reflecting the broader transformation of American society. During the early years of the 20th century extensive moral discussion took place leading up to the creation by AICPA, then called the American Institute of Accountants (AIA), of the formal code of ethics in 1917. The focus of this discussion was on how accountants should conduct themselves rather than on written rules of conduct:

> *... an emphasis upon the correct character of the accountant and the appropriate state of mind he should adopt towards his fellow members, clients and the public. The rhetoric is replete with exhortations of duty, responsibility and loyalty and references to education, upbringing and to the ten commandments* (Preston *et al.*, 1995, p.513).

Preston *et al.* (1995, p.511) also discuss the importance of individual professionals being seen as 'ethical subjects':

> *This early period [1905–1917] concentrated on 'character', notions of the practitioner's correct 'state of mind' and actions 'becoming' of a professional. ... the focus of accountants' ethics in this period was on forming oneself as an ethical subject, and insisting on good character as the basis for legitimating the activities of accountants.*

A number of themes, which featured in the discourse surrounding the US code of ethics at the turn of the 20th century, persisted into the 1980s. However, there were far fewer references to the character of the accountant and no mention of the ten commandments, nor of duty and responsibility.

> *Instead, there were references to the image of the profession, the importance of public relations and/or reducing the expectations gap between what the profession claims to practice and what the public expects of the profession* (Preston *et al.*, 1995, p.514).

Similarly, the professional discourse in Canada (Everett *et al.*, 2005) emphasised morality, character, honesty, reliability, virtue and duty in the first half of the 20th century. Neu *et al.* (2003) examined editorials in the Canadian professional accountancy body's journal over 88 years from 1911 to 1999. They found extensive usage of character-based ethical discussions in the earlier period examined (1911 – 1944). This borrowed heavily from Christian and biblical ideas and appealed to the Protestant work ethic. This discourse drew upon the notion of a 'calling' and the ideal moral character.

> *...character-based ethical discourses were both prominent and grounded in religious discourses of the times. The character-based ethical discourse found in editorials during this period highlighted notions of character, calling, service and work in order to indirectly define norms of ethical conduct. This framing relied heavily on religious ideas: equating professional membership with belonging to a religious order, imbuing the associational founding with mythical origins, and emphasising one's internal moral compass as the true source of ethical behaviour* (Neu *et al.*, 2003, p.83).

Although the religious fervour of the initial period was replaced by more secular expression, many of the same ideas persisted in the second period examined (1945 – 1963), which Neu *et al.* described as *the period of cautious optimism.* These character-based ideas continued to be important in the third and fourth periods examined (1964 – 1979 and 1980 - 1999):

> *Integrity was used as a distilled version of the whole range of pre-war character-based ethical descriptions – moral soundness, honesty, honour, virtue, hard work, discipline and relentless self-examination* (Neu *et al.*, 2003, p.99).

Neu and T'aerien (2000) identify three ways in which the contemporary interest in ethics is positioned *vis-a-vis* the ethical history of the profession. The first argues that while ethics has always been important, changed circumstances require changed ethics. The second looks backward to the time when ethics was the cornerstone of professional practice and urges a 'back to basics' policy for the profession. The third approach is a functionalist one, which asserts that ethics has always been, and continues to be, central to the profession. However, the literature suggests that these assertions are observed more in public utterances than in practical applications. For example, ethical discourses play a role in effacing problems of practice in the UK (Preston *et al.*, 1995; Sikka and Willmott 1995), and in the US (Neu and Saleem, 1996). In relation to Canada, Neu and T'aerien (2000, p.205) stated:

> *... the notion of ethics has a reassuring sound to it. While savings and loan debacles, audit failures, insider trading scandals make visible the fallibility and culpability of accountants and accountancy, discourse of ethics efface these 'problems of practice'.*

Neu and T'aerien concluded, based on narrative illustrations provided from different periods of the Canadian profession's early history, that discussion on ethics was circular, narrow and quite oblivious of the broader social issues such as a series of bank failures and the First World War.

Changes have occurred over time in what the profession considers to be ethical. For example, in 1894 the American Association of Public Accountants (AAPA) prohibited advertising by members. By 1909 five prohibited activities were listed by the AAPA and procedures for adjudicating complaints and imposing penalties were established (Moriarity, 2000). By 1917, the AIA adopted a set of rules of professional conduct. Further rules were added over the years and by 1962 the rules were rearranged as a Code of Professional Ethics. Characteristics of ethical behaviour that were considered important in the early 1990s in the recruitment decisions of accountancy firms, were identified in Ahadiat and Mackie (1993) as: honesty and reliability; honouring the public trust and interest; trustworthiness; avoiding conflicts of interest; broader societal characteristics such as eschewing racism; and operational characteristics such as adhering to firm policies and procedures.

Preston *et al.* (1995, p.535) argued that by the late 20th century, the scope of accountants' morality appeared to be defined by and limited to rules and their increasingly precise interpretation:

> *The rules of the code resonate with a regulatory or legalistic rhetoric and contain a specificity which seeks to both more precisely delineate the extent of the accountants' obligations and to act as a benchmark from which malfeasance may be judged.*

In the context of public practice, three characteristics have been prioritised over all others: independence, objectivity and integrity. However, these characteristics are intangible and resist rigorous definition. One of the responses of the UK and Irish profession to recent public criticisms of the accountancy profession was to delegate responsibility for ethical guidance to the independent Auditing Practices Board (APB), which operates within the Financial Reporting Council structure. Given the widespread belief that many of the early 21st century financial scandals were facilitated, at least, by over-emphasis on rules, the APB set about establishing ethical standards for auditors by focusing on general principles supporting the independence, objectivity and integrity of external auditors and those providing assurance services (APB, 2004). A principles-based approach does not suggest there are no rules. It means that rules are to be adopted by reference to objectives, rather than suggesting that following rules to the letter is what is required to deliver a professional service. Following comprehensive descriptions of independence, objectivity and integrity, the APB guidance identifies threats to these primary concepts and possible safeguards against those threats:

> *If the audit engagement partner identifies threats to the auditors' objectivity, including any perceived loss of independence, he or she should identify and assess the effectiveness of the available safeguards and apply such safeguards as are sufficient to eliminate the threats or reduce them to an acceptable level* (APB, 2004, ES1, Para 36).

Ethical decision-making

In order to evaluate and discuss 'ethics and the professional firm', it is necessary to analyse decision-making from an ethical or moral perspective. Professional firms affect their stakeholder groups as a result of decisions to provide services to particular clients, to design and effect work programmes, and to form and communicate expert opinions on financial, accounting and other issues. To the extent that these decisions are ethical or unethical, accounting firms behave ethically or unethically.

General models of ethical decision-making processes are discussed in the literature (eg.. Shafer *et al.*, 2001; Thorne, 1998; Jones, 1991). Rest *et al.* (1999) and Hunt and Vitell (1986) agree that for moral decision-making processes to be invoked, there must be recognition that a particular decision has a moral dimension. Mayper *et al.* (2005) demonstrate that ethical sensitivity (or recognition) is a pre-requisite for the application of ethical judgement. Ethical behaviour requires more than the ability to make a moral or ethical judgement. An intention to behave correctly must follow the judgement, in addition to acting on this intention. Models of ethical decision-making (including Thorne, 1998; Jones, 1991; Rest, 1983) generally include four components, as follows:

(i) Recognise a moral issue;
(ii) Make a moral or ethical judgement;
(iii) Establish moral intent or behavioural intentions; and
(iv) Engage in moral behaviour.

These four components are influenced by the 'perceived moral intensity' of the issue under consideration, which should influence all components of the ethical decision-making process. According to Jones (1991), moral intensity is multi-dimensional and its components include:

- magnitude of consequences;
- probability of effect;
- temporal immediacy;
- social consensus;
- proximity; and
- concentration of effect.

Drawing on prior research to demonstrate that moral intensity affects recognition of a moral issue by its impact on the individual's capacity to recognise the consequences of a decision, Mayper *et al.* (2005, p.40) explain how it influences:

> *...the salience and vividness of the effects of a moral issue. Salience concerns how moral issues stand out from the backgrounds (Jones 1991, 380). Vividness deals with how moral issues create emotion, are concrete, create images, or invoke a sense of proximity.*

Shafer *et al.* (2001) argue that higher levels of moral intensity should act as a deterrent to unethical intentions among auditors. This deterrent would be reinforced by the perceived threat of sanctions from professional bodies.

> *...as the perceived magnitude of potential losses to financial statement users and the perceived likelihood of those losses occurring increases, the assessed likelihood of formal sanctions such as litigation and disciplinary actions from professional organisations should also increase* (Shafer *et al.*, 2001, p.260).

To illustrate the relevance of their model in an audit firm-related context, Shafer *et al.* (2001) suggest how different aspects of moral intensity are related to aspects of client pressure on an auditor to acquiesce in aggressive financial reporting. This is summarised in Table 2.1.

Table 2.1 Auditor pressure to acquiesce in aggressive financial reporting by components of moral intensity

Components of moral intensity:	**Aggressive financial reporting analysed:**
Magnitude of consequences	Potential losses to financial statement users. Disciplinary sanction.
Probability of effect	Likelihood of consequences actually occurring.
Temporal immediacy	The shorter the time between the action and consequences occurring, the greater the moral intensity.
Social consensus	Greater consensus leads to greater moral intensity. Situations involving clear violations of professional standards should be more morally intense than situations in 'grey areas'.
Proximity	Affinity of auditor to victims or beneficiaries (long-term client with business development potential versus anonymous shareholders).
Concentration of effect	If the effect of a financial statement misstatement is concentrated on a single investor or creditor, the moral intensity is greater.

Adapted from: Shafer *et al.* (2001, p.258-9)

However, Mayper *et al.* (2005) argue that the traditional focus on accounting as a primarily technical discipline desensitises entrants to the profession to the moral aspects of their work, thus making it difficult for accountants to make moral judgements. Professionals focused on performing their professional tasks tend to filter out the moral implications that are part of the decision context. This 'technicist approach' (Mayper *et al.*, 2005, p.37) compounds the negative effects of 'corporate hegemony (the domination of business values in all areas of human life)' on students' and practitioners' abilities to recognise ethical dimensions of problems or to prioritise the moral over the economic aspects.

Ethical codes

Ethical codes have been defined in a number of ways. A useful working definition in the context of the accountancy profession, is provided by Frankel (1989, p.110), as follows:

> *A profession's code of ethics is perhaps its most visible and explicit enunciation of its professional norms. A code embodies the collective conscience of a profession and is testimony to the group's recognition of its moral dimension.*

According to Abbott (1983), ethical codes are the most concrete cultural form in which professions acknowledge their societal obligations. However, a recurrent theme in the accounting literature is that codes are massaged over time and used by the profession to legitimate their activities and/or defend their privileged status (Citron, 2003; Preston *et al.*, 1995). They have often been perceived to be cynical exercises in public relations. Parker (1994) argues that ethical codes seek to combat inequality in society while at the same time preserving inequality through their justification of professional privilege.

Moreover, it has been argued that professional ideology, as embodied in a code of ethics, is converted into a form of social power that can be wielded in the interests of the profession and to the benefit or detriment of the public interest (Parker, 1994). Citron (2003, p.248) argues that the development of the UK ethical guidance in the 1990s illustrated 'an exercise of power by the profession in order to promote its own worldview regarding the nature and scope of ethical audit behaviour.' Frankel (1989) refers to the potential for codes to have 'dysfunctions' such as manipulating public impression, redefining the profession's collective responsibility, reinforcing alienation towards broader social values and alienation between an organisation's hierarchy and ordinary members. Brinkmann and Ims (2003) identify conditions within the environment and processes, which, in turn, promote either positive or negative effects of ethical codes. These conditions are set out in Table 2.2.

Table 2.2 Conditions determining whether a code has positive or negative effects

Conditions which further positive code effects, i.e. code functions:	**Types of mediating conditions (understandable as a sequence of stages):**	**Conditions which further negative code effects, ie. code dysfunctions:**
Openness and honesty	Organisation climate	Pessimism, cynicism
Idealistic, inner directed	Code intentions and objective	Defensive, reactive, outer-directed
Participatory, bottom-up	Code creation and procedure	Administrative, top-down
Simple and abstract elements	Code content	Sophisticated, detailed elements
Stimulation of dialogue	Code implementation, use and administration	Individual lip-service adjustment, blocking of dialogue and problem sharing

Source: Brinkmann and Ims (2003, p.268)

Ethical Code Objectives

The purpose of ethics in business and accounting is to direct people to abide by a code of conduct that facilitates and encourages public confidence in their products and services (Smith, 2003), to facilitate professional self-control as well as to express and strengthen the community orientation of profession members (Parker, 1994). Frankel (1989) classified ethical codes as aspirational, educational and regulatory and he listed the following eight functions as defining the role of codes:

- enabling documents;
- sources of public evaluation;
- media of professional socialisation;
- enhancement of a profession's reputation and public trust;
- preservation of entrenched professional biases;
- deterrent to unethical behaviour;
- support system; and
- adjudication.

Building on Frankel's (1989) characterisation, Brinkmann and Ims (2003) identify six main functions of ethical codes, as set out in Table 2.3. They distinguish between intended and positive functions, and latent and negative functions in a three-by-two matrix based on the educational, regulatory and aspirational classification of codes.

Table 2.3 Six main functions of ethical codes

	Intended and positive:	Latent and negative:
Educational	Increase individual moral awareness and behaviour	Assume and reinforce pre-conventionalism, cynicism, outer-directness
Regulatory	Recognise moral conflicts and help with resolving them	Hinder necessary/possible learning of conflict handling by dialogue
Aspirational	Communicate ideals for individuals and collective conscience (moral climate)	Window dressing, covering up/concealing a disputable practice

Source: Brinkmann and Ims (2003, p.268)

A functionalist model of codes of ethics suggests that codes serve to ensure and protect clients' interests in an engagement where professionals deliver expert services, the quality of which cannot easily be judged or measured (Preston *et al.*, 1995). Such a claim is normally accompanied by claims for exclusive rights to practice. Where these are supported by explicit or implicit ethical codes, the public interest is said to be served both by the professional regulation of members and by protecting the public from unscrupulous and unqualified practitioners (Preston *et al.*, 1995). The functionalist model of ethics, often used by the professions in their official histories and public relations activities, suggests that the accountancy profession exercises a community-delegated authority to license and discipline its members (Parker, 1994).

A critical interpretation of the functionalist model argues that a code of ethics is one of a number of means used by the profession to secure privileges for its members (see for example, Mitchell *et al.*, 1993; Willmott, 1986). This view claims that beneath the overt public interest claims is a submerged private interest agenda.

Symbolic Nature of Ethical Codes

In addition to serving structural-functional purposes (Neu, 1991), including providing guidance for ethical conflict resolution (Reynolds, 2000; Brinkmann, 2002), a number of studies have examined the symbolic nature of ethical codes and the use of such codes in legitimating the activities of accountants (for example, Citron, 2003; Preston *et al.*, 1995; Mitchell, *et al.*, 1994; Parker, 1994; and Sawyer, 1991).

It has been argued that the potential contradictions between accountancy as a profession and as a commercial enterprise can cause leaders in the profession to pursue legitimating activities (Radcliffe *et al.*, 1994; Willmott *et al.*, 1993). Preston *et al.* also argue that the promulgation of professional codes of ethics confers legitimacy upon a professional body. Preston *et al.* (1995, p.510) explain how the terms legitimacy and legitimation are used in the prior literature in the context of accountants' professionalisation processes, as follows:

> *Typically, legitimacy and legitimation are conceived of in terms of accountants' continual quest to secure professional privileges. Legitimacy is conceived as congruence between institutional actions and social values and legitimation as actions that institutions take either to signal value congruency or to change social values.*

Neu (1991) explains the legitimation process as one by which the profession attempts to justify its right to exist to the State, other institutions, the general public and its members. He argues that accountancy is not the only profession to engage in legitimation activities. However, because of the diversity of users and the visibility of services provided by the accountancy profession, accountancy differs in its need to convince uninformed users that accountants can be trusted and are legitimate. Neu argues that the profession uses impression management to this end. He concludes that the accounting profession's rules for professional conduct, including its codes of ethics, provide a written justification for arguing that accountants are ethically superior to other individuals (eg.. those pursuing purely commercial interests) and 'thus should be trusted in the sphere of financial matters' (Neu, 1991, p.303).

Citron (2003) illustrates how the UK Chartered Accountants Joint Ethics Committee's Statement on *Integrity, Objectivity and Independence* in 1996 provided legitimation for the profession's increased commercial activities. He concluded, based on an examination of discussion papers preceding the 1996 Statement, of the wording of the Statement itself, and of responses by 58 organisations and individuals, that the new statement:

> *...[R]eflects and indeed helps promote this increased commercialisation, while at the same time seeking to maintain an acceptable level of credibility for the profession in the eyes of the public* (Citron, 2003, p.267).

Whilst arguing that ethical codes operate largely in the private interest, Parker (1994) concedes that they also have a constructive and socialising impact upon accountants. Higgins and Olson (1972, cited in Preston *et al.*, 1995) claim that agreement on ethical concepts and adherence to them by an overwhelming majority of practitioners transforms an occupation into a profession.

Enforcement of Ethical Codes

Disciplinary sanctions are a significant tool available to the accounting profession to encourage members to follow a uniform approach to the ethical practice of accounting (Shafer *et al.*, 2001; Moriarity, 2000). For 'functionalists', professional peers are considered to be best equipped to determine satisfactory performance because of the assumed inability of the 'consumer' to judge the quality of expertise provided by the practitioner (Bédard, 2001). Bédard (p.402) explains that codes of ethics and disciplinary enforcement:

> *...are not there to control the 'peculiarly exploitative opportunities' (Goode, 1957, p.196) resulting from the asymmetry of expertise, but to 'legitimize the autonomy of the professions and ensure their independence from outside scrutiny and control' (Parker, 1994, p.516). They represent a public relations effort by the profession to convince users that accountants can be trusted and thereby establish its legitimacy and maintain its privileges.*

In the context of professional disciplinary activities, tensions can arise between a profession's pursuit of autonomy and the public's demand for accountability (Frankel, 1989). The protective and status-preserving motives for the framing of disciplinary rules by early professional associations of accountants is highlighted in Walker (1996). Other studies have raised doubts about the ongoing ability of accounting bodies to effectively regulate major firms. The literature points to limitations in disciplinary activity against professional firms undertaken by professional bodies (see eg.. Mitchell *et al.* (1994) who analyse the Polly Peck case and investigation by ICAEW of its auditors, Coopers & Lybrand; Canning and O'Dwyer (2003) who investigate the 'ethics machinery' of ICAI following from public criticisms of accountants' roles in scandals uncovered by government-appointed tribunals of enquiry in Ireland in the 1990s). See also Canning and O'Dwyer (2001); Sikka (2001b); Rollins and Bremser (1997); Sikka and Willmott (1995); Mitchell *et al.* (1994). Evidence is provided in this literature of a contradiction between rhetoric and practice in the context of the profession pursuing deviant behaviour. In particular, it is argued that big firms avoid sanctions by adopting delaying tactics in the face of adverse rulings by professional body disciplinary procedures (see eg.. Arnold and Sikka, 2001; Sikka, 2001a; and Mitchell *et al.*, 2000). Moreover, Rollins and Bremser (1997, p.204) explain the status of larger firms in the context of regulatory enforcement as follows:

> *Institutional theory predicts that brand name auditors will be treated differently by a regulatory agency. Brand name auditors have formal structures, policies and procedures to demonstrate conformity to institutional rules and constituent expectations, and they have greater auditing experience than most no-name brand auditing firms. They have attained a certain amount of social legitimacy and power. There is a logic of confidence associated with brand name auditors which has influenced the capital markets and regulators.*

The literature refers to the limited evidence of audit firms being held accountable. Canning and O'Dwyer (2003) report perceptions that big firms cannot be adequately disciplined by professional bodies as they contribute large proportions of their funding. In reports of State investigations, such as America's SEC, the UK's Department of Trade and Industry (DTI), and Ireland's Tribunals of Enquiry, the evidence shows that the profession has failed to adequately discipline the auditing firms involved (Rollins and Bremser, 1997; Mitchell *et al.*, 1994). Bédard (2001) refers to the existing research in Anglo-Saxon countries showing a primacy of private interest over public interest in the accountancy profession disciplinary enforcement systems. For example, Mitchell *et al.* (1994) lists UK accountancy firms criticised in DTI Inspectors' reports covering the period 1967–1989. These cases were taken from the limited number of reports published, and all sizes of audit firm featured. Mitchell *et al.* argue that, because one of the inspectors in these investigations is usually a partner in a big firm, the objectivity of DTI inspector reports is suspect. A flaw in the process is perceived to be the inter-reliance of the State and the profession. On the one hand, the State grants a monopoly for audit services to specified accountancy bodies. On the other, the DTI uses as inspectors, partners in firms which have been the subject of other investigations. The State also has an interest in promoting confidence in the objectivity of audited financial reports and as trust plays a crucial role in financial information for capital markets, it is argued that the State has an interest in not exposing the 'dirty underbelly'.

Similarly, research analysing Accounting and Auditing Enforcement Releases (AAERs) promulgated by the SEC over the 11 years 1987–1997 (Beasley, Carcello and Hermanson 1999) was criticised by Briloff (2001, p.126) on the grounds that the data used was not representative of the 'really stinking stuff which is contaminating the accounting and financial reporting environment'. His argument was that the sample companies in the research were not the companies regularly criticised in the business press under such accusing headlines as 'Earning Hocus-Pocus' and 'Where were the accountants?', both of which appeared as part of a special edition of *Business Week* entitled 'Who can you trust?' in 1989. Briloff independently investigated AAERs issued between 1987 and 1998, thereby including an additional year over the Releases investigated in the Beasley *et al.* (1999) study. He concluded that there was a bias in the regulatory process. He maintained that Big 8/6/5 firms were treated leniently by the SEC. Briloff maintained that even where audit firms were obviously associated with high profile public concern cases, they were treated in a very benign way or not cited at all. In a particular case involving a then Big 6 Firm, Briloff was particularly critical of the regulator blaming the individual auditor rather than the firm, arguing that the repeated use of the phrase 'Withers caused Coopers and Lybrand to …' was 'rubbish' (Briloff, 2001, p.129). Briloff acknowledged that the individual auditor failed in his professional duty in the particular case, but his argument was that the SEC effectively made a scapegoat out of the individual auditor while minimising the role of the firm (Briloff, 2001). From the evidence available, Briloff concluded that the unprofessional and unethical behaviour of the engagement partner was consistent with the 'tone at the top' of the firm.

Summary

The importance of professional ethics to accountancy has been discussed in its historical context in this chapter. The literature suggests that a tension exists between the sense of social responsibility (to fellow members and to the public at large) engendered by traditional professionalism with individual members and member firms subscribing to professional ethics, and the use and abuse by some contemporary practitioners of the commonly held respect for professions in a cynical way to promote self-interest. The literature reviewed in chapters one and two provides a framework against which the actions of professional firms can be evaluated from an ethical perspective. The combination of a heritage anchored in earning and maintaining a reputation for independence, honesty, objectivity and integrity, and expert skills in financial matters, leads to expectations of accountants in general, and accounting firms in particular, that they prioritise the public interest above self-interest. This prioritisation leads to an expectation that reports and advice provided by accounting firms is trustworthy. The literature emphasises that the consequences of accounting firms losing the public trust are substantial. The profession has already lost one of its prized hallmarks, ie. its right to self-regulate (Brown, 2005; Boyd, 2004). In the context of ethics and the professional firm, Staubus (2005) provides a concise description of the major flaw which exerts pressure on the ethicality of some accounting firm practices. In the crucial tri-party corporate governance relationship involving shareholders, management and external auditors, the system offers:

> *... temptations to behave unethically by favouring the interests of client managements over those of the investing public, thus compromising the integrity and effectiveness of the financial reporting system that is so important to those societies that depend on relatively free capital markets* (Staubus, 2005, p.11).

In order to cope with the potential conflicts created by the demands of the public interest orientation of public accounting practice and responding to the commercial opportunities presented by economic and technological developments, the literature suggests that accounting practitioners walk a narrow ethical line. Some of the inevitable falls from grace are identified in chapter three, where ethical dilemmas and challenges experienced by accounting firms and identified in the literature are discussed.

Chapter Three

Ethical Dilemmas and Challenges

> *If societal values are deteriorating, maintaining high ethical standards in accounting and business grows increasingly difficult. Many will undoubtedly ask: If everyone else is cheating, then how can an ethical person possibly succeed? The answer depends on the definition of success* (Smith, 2003, p.48).

Introduction

The history of the accounting profession and the importance of reputation, trust and ethicality to accountants, and accounting firms, were discussed in the earlier chapters of this report. Moreover, the expansion of the sphere of influence of accounting firms was alluded to in the context of a professionalisation process that took place over 150 years during which accountants increasingly formalised their occupational grouping and their control over specific professional activities. Over this period of time (mid-19th century to date), accountants were portrayed in the literature as engaging in legitimising activities such as creating and maintaining a professional image by strenuously defending their right to self-regulation, appealing to the centrality of ethical codes to their philosophy and practice, and espousing a public interest focus. Zeff (2003b) described the US profession as reaching the height of its influence around the mid-1960s, while the 1980s saw a substantial increase in critical questioning of the *modus operandi,* power and motives of the UK profession.

In this chapter, specific pressures on the ideals of professionalism identified in the literature as affecting, or created by, accountancy firms, are discussed. The overarching theme is the extent to which the responses by accounting firms to available commercial opportunities exerted pressure on the traditional core values of independence, objectivity and integrity. The literature argues that the firms exposed themselves to valid accusations of 'desecrating their covenant with society' (Briloff, 1990) because they failed to prioritise the public interest over self-interest. Self-interest is shown in the literature to be pursued by accounting firms without adequately or objectively acknowledging or dealing with the threats posed to the profession's core values. The three traditional characteristics of auditors and, by association, of accountancy firms (independence, objectivity and integrity) have been shown to be valued by and valuable to accountants. They are the core personal attributes, which, combined with competence and expertise, justify the State-granted monopoly over the mandatory audit for registered companies. They also underpin demand for many other services which accounting firms are competent to discharge.

The chapter concludes with a brief exploration of the rules-based culture that the literature argues has become endemic in public accounting practice and financial reporting. The influence of a rules culture on moral sensitivity and its potential for diminishing the status and quality of the accounting profession is discussed in the final section of this chapter.

Ethical dilemmas

Ethical dilemmas for professional practitioners are a fact of life (Leung and Cooper, 1995). In the context of accounting firms, these dilemmas arise when there are conflicting demands or opportunities in the course of delivering the expert services offered by professional firms (Stumpf *et al.*, 2002). There is some evidence in the literature that auditors appear to define ethical dilemmas in terms of the rules of professional conduct and can more easily identify dilemmas that fall within those rules (see eg. Jones *et al.*, 2003). However the critical and ethics literatures identify a broader set of potential conflicts encountered by external auditors in the context of their unique responsibility to shareholders who frequently evaluate the integrity of financial reports by reference to the external auditor's opinion on those statements.

In this section, the dilemmas faced or created by accounting firms in pursuit of developing and maintaining their 'occupational authority' (West, 2003), reputation and status as moral practitioners of high integrity (Herron and Gilbertson, 2004; Francis, 1990) are examined.

Commercial pressures on professionalism

> *Complexities and volatilities in commercial activity, incentives and propensities for secrecy and obfuscation, conflicting interests among affected parties and the severity of the consequences of misjudgements conspire to ensure that the lot of an accounting professional is not an easy one* (West, 2003, p.193).

Commercial pressures on the ideals of professionalism in the past four or five decades include the corporate merger movement of the 1960s and the related rationalisation of the accounting profession. From an ethical and traditional public practice point of view, the consequences of these events are potentially dysfunctional. Dysfunctional consequences for accounting firms include prioritising client satisfaction over professional standards and reputation, and fee/profit maximisation over audit quality. Moreover, commercial opportunities, such as providing non-audit services (NAS) or management advisory services (MAS), arising from expanded and more complex business activities threaten, both perceived and real, auditor independence.

Pressures emanating from the corporate merger movement of the 1960s contributed to stresses on the 'ability of audit firms to maintain a high level of professional integrity independent of these market forces' (Boyd, 2004, p.380). Merging corporations retained only one of the two previous auditors and successive mergers of audit firms reduced client loyalty. Pressure to deliver improved earnings led to corporate opposition to constraints on freedom to select accounting methods. 'Opinion shopping' among clients became popular and audit firms were perceived to be complicit in helping clients escape the adverse effects of professional pronouncements[1] (Young, 2005; Boyd, 2004; McMillan, 2004; Reinstein and McMillan, 2004; Zeff, 2003b). Zeff (2003b, p.203) describes the intensity of audit partner efforts to accommodate client wishes in the context of a culture shift within professional practice, as follows:

> *A gradual development within the Big Eight firms during the 1980s was a significant shift in the posture of audit partners toward their clients, probably spurred by their perceived pressure to retain valued clients. In previous years, partners conveyed a firm position on the propriety of any borderline accounting and disclosure practices adopted by the client, but increasingly in the 1980s partners would be seen huddling with the firm's technical specialists to find any means – perhaps restructuring a major vehicle, reconfiguring a transaction, or straining to rationalise the application of a suitable analogy - to enable the firm to approve the accounting treatment sought by the client.*

Pressures on professional ideals also emanated from merger activity within the profession itself from the 1960s (Boyd, 2004; Zeff, 2003c). Briloff (1990, p.26) was very critical of the rationalisation trend in the 1970s and 1980s of the major accountancy firms (from Big Eight to Big Five at that time), suggesting that the objective of the exercise was to achieve:

> *...bigger gross revenues, more concentrated power, probably bigger muscles to push out competition from various management advisory and consultative enterprises.*

According to Boyd (2004), the domination of power and concentration in ownership evident in the global accountancy profession was without parallel in any other profession.

In addition to the profession responding to commercial opportunities with increased industrial concentration (Beattie *et al.*, 2003) and substantially increased manpower, the big firms also reorganised themselves in a more business-like structure, which reflected a greater emphasis on client satisfaction than on maintaining traditional distance in support of objectivity (Stumpf *et al.*, 2002). This phenomenon is illustrated by the following extract from Boyd (2004, p.394):

> *According to KPMG's 1997-1998 Annual Report in the United Kingdom, that firm had moved from a product-based form of organisational design, in which the audit division was normally separate from the consulting division on the firm's organisation chart, to a market-oriented form of organisational structure, in which all services to particular market sectors were grouped together in industry-specific divisions ... likely at the cost of yet more pressures on audit independence.*

The literature provides conflicting views on the inevitability of the commercial and capital market pressures and accounting firm responses to cause an extreme consequence (Brown, 2005; Boyd, 2004; Wilson, 2002). Wilson (2002, cited in Reinstein and McMillan, 2004, p.955), opined that a 'perfect storm' occurred between 1996 and 2000, during which:

> *...a concurrence of unpredictable, rare and unusual conditions ... combined to create a unique, devastating event [Enron debacle].*

He characterised this period (cited in Reinstein and McMillan, 2004, p.955) as presenting:

> *...an unparalleled opportunity to inadvertently or intentionally misrepresent information. Business risk was at an all time high, the underlying activities were remarkably difficult to measure reliably, and there were very strong incentives to manipulate reported numbers.*

However, Boyd (2004, p.377), argues that the systemic failure to note and correct the increasing range of new conflicts of interest brought about by this extreme industrial concentration in the last quarter of the 20th century led to:

> *...intolerable pressures on the ethical judgements of experienced professionals employed by accounting firms that presumably otherwise espoused adherence to the highest levels of ethical integrity.*

Somewhat earlier, Hanlon (1994) had explored the commercialisation of the profession. He provides valuable insights into the impact of intensified competition for audit business between accountancy firms and the growing importance of non-audit business as a source of revenue and audit as a vehicle for securing other more lucrative business. Hanlon's work, based on questionnaires completed by members of one chartered institute of accountants, and interviews with trainee accountants in audit and industry, and with partners in the then Big Six firms, has been criticised (Dezalay, 1997; Willmott and Sikka, 1997) for not exploring adequately other drivers of the commercialisation process, such as the State and powerful clients. Willmott and Sikka (1997) argue that economic restructuring of the last quarter of the 20th century presented accountants and other expert labour groups with opportunities, while at the same time restricting the life chances of many others. While they accept Hanlon's (1997) thesis that accounting firms have enthusiastically embraced the opportunities presented by the enterprise culture of that period, they criticise him (p.836) for not addressing what they describe as a 'global understanding of the pressures promoting the commercialisation of accounting', identifying them as:

- the balance of power between finance and industry generated demands for financial engineering, 'creative accounting', junk bonds, derivatives, options *etc.*, because large corporations were increasingly generating profits from financial speculation;
- high profile failures and financial scandals creating concerns about the scale of losses; and
- accountancy firms exploiting opportunities to offer broader assurance services, thereby increasing 'accounting think' in the process.

Moreover, Willmott and Sikka (1997, p.837) argue that given the broadening scope of marketing activities and services provided by large accounting firms, and their global reach, they are credited by some with actively disseminating western capitalist culture in 'Eastern, Pacific, Asian and African economies to enable capital roam the world and (re)organise global and local economic space on highly unequal terms.'

Some issues relating to the drivers and impact of changes in professional norms have yet to be addressed in an accounting context. Although there is some evidence in the legal literature to suggest that clients attempt to dominate corporate lawyers and force them to provide certain services which prioritise commercial issues and profit, this area has yet to be addressed in relation to accountants (Hanlon, 1997). Empirical studies focusing on medicine indicate that corporatisation shifts the primary norms from quality care and service in the public interest to organisational objectives such as cost containment and profit maximisation (Alexander and D'Aunno, 1990). Similarly this concept has been discussed in the legal profession as more lawyers are employed in multidisciplinary practices under the control of non-professionals or professionals who are not lawyers (see Lucci, 2003; Shafer *et al.*, 2002).

Commercial ethos of accountancy firms

Willmott and Sikka (1997) argue that in addition to the big accounting firms resembling multinational companies in their size and structures, they increasingly adopt a commercial ethos as distinct from a traditional professional culture. Hanlon (1997) refers to the long-standing tensions between the commercial side of accountancy firms (tax, management services, corporate finance *etc.*) and the 'public-oriented" audit side of professional practices. These tensions between professionalism and commercialisation have been investigated in the literature (eg. Boyd, 2004; Radcliffe *et al.*, 1994). Such investigation aims to achieve:

> *...critical appreciation of the provision of accounting services and in particular, of the claims of accountancy institutions to provide independent and useful services and thereby to offer a socially valuable activity*' (Radcliffe *et al.*, 1994, p.602).

Radcliffe *et al.* (1994, p.602) describe the 'professional enterprise of accountancy' as follows:

> *On the one hand, accountancy can be presented in terms that would be familiar to those who have examined the traits of professions, focusing on attributes such as commitment to a service ideal, self-regulation, ethical behaviour, specialised training and expertise. Accountancy's claims to professionalism are made in*

> *the context of counterclaims regarding the abuse of monopoly power, unethical behaviour and partisan commitments to major corporations. Yet, on the other hand, accountancy is also presented as a commercial or enterprising activity, with accountancy firms pursuing profit and growth, seeking new markets and products. From a commercial perspective, the profession's aggregate activity can be thought of as an accounting industry with competition to supply services both within the profession, and between accountancy and other groups.*

Hanlon (1994, p.121, cited in Wilmott and Sikka, 1997, p.832) explains that accounting firms have been placing increasing emphasis on the commercial acumen of their staff:

> *...a firm like ours is a commercial organisation and the bottom line is that ... First of all the individual must contribute to the profitability of the business. In part, that is bringing in business but essentially profitability is based upon the ability to serve existing clients well* (Big Six Director quoted in Hanlon, 1994, p.121).

Gendron (2002, p.664) provides a concise description of the tensions between 'professional and commercial logics of action' in the context of audit practice. Using the prior literature, Gendron also identifies 'ideal types' within these competing cultures and analyses the ideal type by organisational components such as audit pricing strategy, service differentiation strategy, and attitudes etc., and by client-acceptance decision processes. Tables 3.1 and 3.2 reproduce Gendron's characterisations.

Table 3.1 'Ideal types' based on audit firm organisational components

Organizational component	Professional logic	Commercial logic
Practice-development strategy:		
Audit pricing strategy	Charge for audit services is similar to standard price (it is considered that discounts depreciate the value of auditing in the eyes of clients and society)	Charge for audit services is significantly discounted (it is considered that being auditor facilitates the sale of other services to auditees)
Service differentiation strategy	Centred on the firm's reputation of expertise	Centred on the development of close relationships with auditees
Partner-compensation scheme:		
Main aspect emphasised in determining partner compensation	Expertise (practice-development performance is not emphasised in order not to compromise partner's independence)	Practice development performance (it is believed that emphasis on this aspect increases partners' sensitivity to profitability)

Source: Gendron (2002, p.667)

Table 3.1 'Ideal types' based on audit firm organisational components (Continued)

Organizational Component	Professional logic	Commercial logic
System of management by objectives:		
Nature of objectives taken into account	A broad range of long-term objectives are firstly considered	Short-term objectives related to profitability and growth are firstly considered
Client acceptance policies	Centred on collegiality and protection of third parties' interests	Centred on profit considerations
Attitudes of participants:		
Identification with the profession	Higher	Lower
Main objective of audit work	Serving the public	Making profits within a short to middle term horizon
Main source of motivation when practicing	Challenge to carry out audit engagements	Remuneration
Importance given to independence	Higher	Lower

Source: Gendron (2002, p.667)

Table 3.2 'Ideal types' based on client-acceptance decision process

Dimension of client-acceptance decision	**Professional logic**	**Commercial logic**
Dominant source(s) of motivation in accepting new clients	Challenge to apply auditing expertise to new situations, and the possibility of (further) developing the firm's reputation	Remuneration
Emphasis on key issues that are claimed to be central to the profession in accepting new clients (i.e. firm staffing, expertise, and independence)	Higher	Lower (since these issues are perceived by commercial auditors as not being closely related to profitability)
Main audit stakeholders about whom partnerships are concerned	Public and third parties	Potential client's management (who largely influences audit renewals and is in charge of giving consulting engagements to the firm)

Source: Gendron (2002, p.667)

Table 3.2 'Ideal types' based on client-acceptance decision process (Continued)

Dimension of client-acceptance decision	Professional logic	Commercial logic
Importance given to spin-off work	Lower (in order not to compromise independence)	Higher (since spin-off work is very lucrative)

Source: Gendron (2002, p.667)

It has been argued that the globalisation of the large accountancy firms has facilitated clients in their pursuit of global profits (Willmott and Sikka, 1997; Hanlon, 1994). However, Willmott and Sikka (1997) highlight how this 'world structure' can be abandoned by the firms when they are being held accountable across legal jurisdictions. This is illustrated by one of the conclusions of the US Senate investigation into the BCCI scandal, that the partnership structure was inappropriate for international regulatory arrangements (Willmott and Sikka,1997). Sikka and Willmott (1995) refer to the 'supranational pressures' that increasingly condition both the local practice and national standing of professional groups as distinct from inter-professional competition within countries. They argued that within the 'business professions' in the 1980s, inter-professional competition within, and between professions was conditioned by the expanding opportunities for exploiting and regulating the globalisation of trade and the internationalisation of markets for legal, financial and consultancy services.

In the US, the commercial ethos of accounting was reinforced in the late 1990s by the trend of corporate entities such as American Express taking over CPA firms (Shafer *et al.*, 2002). While discussion of corporate ownership of CPA firms in the professional literature initially focused on the threat posed to auditor independence, threats to professionalism and professional ethics were subsequently highlighted (Shafer *et al.*, 2002). The fear expressed is that as the commercial ethos advances within public accounting, strategies are adopted that aim to modify accepted standards of performance. One manifestation of the change in ethos of the accounting profession over the last quarter of the 20th century is the way audit fees have become increasingly subject to competitive forces placing pressures on firms to adopt cost reduction strategies. There is evidence of 'low-balling' where audit firms reduce the audit fee when tendering for new business in the hope or expectation that the 'loss leader' will be compensated by the opportunity to attract other business from the same client (Boyd, 2004; Beattie *et al.*, 2003; Willmott and Sikka, 1997; Economist, 1990).

Threats to professionalism

> *[A] profession is judged by the performance of its practitioners, and a failure on the part of one to meet expectations diminishes the whole* (Magill and Previts, 1991).

It is extensively argued throughout the literature that the accountancy profession responded to the many opportunities offered by economic, regulatory and technological advances of the 20th century by expanding the scope of services they offered, despite the risk of undermining their image as independent, objective professionals of high integrity (see eg. Brown, 2005; Citron, 2003). In fact, it is often argued that they used this image to their advantage:

> *...on the back of the state guaranteed market of auditing, some accountancy firms have become global business and consulting supermarkets* (Sikka, 2004, p.186).

Concerns about the range of services provided by accountancy firms are not new. For example, the Public Oversight Board (1979, p.56) noted:

> *...[T]here is enough concern about the scope of services in responsible quarters so that the question cannot be dismissed as a 'non-problem.' The Board believes that there is potential danger to the public interest and to the profession in the unlimited expansion of MAS to audit clients, and some moderating principles and procedures are needed.*

Changes in the wider society[2] have influenced changes in the accountancy profession's behaviour, largely because of opportunities afforded by these changes to accounting firms to expand their sphere of influence (Velayutham and Rahman, 2000; Willmott and Sikka, 1997). Accounting numbers, with their aura of accuracy and objectivity have increasingly been used to evaluate, monitor and control a broader range of activities in society.

In the 1980s, US CPA firms began promoting themselves, not as auditors who served the interests of the public, but as client-service professionals who solved business problems (Daly and Schuler, 1998). Evidence is provided in Citron (2003) of the relative increase over time in the UK of non-audit fees. Antle (1999) provides similar evidence for the US. Professional journals, such as *Accountancy* regularly report surveys of accountancy firm fees (see, eg. September 2005; 2003 and October 2004 issues detailing trends in non-audit service fees paid by FTSE 100 companies as a proportion of total fees paid to Big Four accounting firms). Beattie and Fearnley (2002, p.*ix*) identify two main concerns associated with auditor independence arising from the relative increase in non-audit fee income, as follows:

> *Auditors may not stand up to management because they wish to retain the additional income from NAS which is in management's gift and, second, the provision of a range of services to management may lead the auditor to identify too closely with management and lose scepticism.*

In addition to expanding the scope of services offered, the literature also describes how accountancy firms recruited both vast numbers of trainees and substantial numbers of non-accounting professionals, and concentrated the 'industry' into a small number of major firms. Many of these trainees subsequently took senior and influential positions with client companies. Their support of the *alma mater* was subsequently encouraged by the firm with which they trained. The creation and perception of multi-disciplinary services' firms is described in the following quotations:

> *Whether intentional or merely driven by market forces, evidence of the accounting profession's movement toward 'one-stop shopping' for professional services abounds. Recently, the American Institute of Certified Public Accountants (AICPA) changed its professional ethics rules to allow up to one-third of the partners at an accounting firm to be non-CPAs. This modification, for the first time, allows sizable ownership interest by non-CPAs, including attorneys. This change has caused CPA firms, and in particular Big Five firms, to greatly enhance their recruitment of leading attorneys in the tax, corporate and estate law areas. Lured in many cases by more money, less pressure to develop new clients and tremendous capital support, some of the legal profession's best and brightest have traded in their partnership keys for the right to a seat at the CPA business table. Ernst & Young, to mention only one, currently counts more than 800 attorneys among its US tax services team, making it second only to the Internal Revenue Service (IRS) in number of attorneys employed* (Robinson, 1999, p.24).

> *Accounting firms ... ... now resemble corporate cafeterias offering a staggering selection of business advisory services, many with little or nothing to do with the profession's traditional core competencies* (Andrew, 1988, p.24, cited in Boyd, 2004, p.384).

Lucci (2003) also analyses the growth in legal services offered by Big Five/Four accountancy firms. The explicit drive by audit firms towards providing all conceivable client services is captured in the following quotation from PricewaterhouseCoopers Canada (1998, cited in Boyd, 2004, p.384):

> *We will truly be a breakaway firm when our clients think of us as always being able to provide them with assistance with virtually any business or industry issue they face.*

Citron (2003) argues that the qualitative change in the nature of audit firms' activities is even more significant than the relative growth in consulting and related activities. He instances the growth in the provision of assurance services as an example of services where the dividing line between traditional audit and MAS is less clear-cut. Services such as risk assessment, systems reliability and entity performance measurement are included in these other assurance services. Elliott (1998), who was a KPMG partner at the time and subsequently became Chairman of AICPA (1999/2000) and chaired its special committee on Assurance Services, argues that these services are rooted in the audit tradition. However, unlike audit, the profession has no monopolistic exclusivity over the provision of these services and must compete for market share.

Early outspoken criticisms of the profession forewarned of events to come at the beginning of the 21st century. For example, Briloff (1990, p.25) characterised the profession as 'without a compass' and its members as determined 'to de-professionalise our pursuit'. In particular, he identified 'a nexus of perversity', including 'the denigration of the independent audit responsibilities of the firm, and those engaged in that activity'. This view has been repeated in recent times in the context of analyses into Enron and other contemporary accounting scandals. See, for example, Zeff (2003b; 2003c) and Wyatt (2004; 2003). A further example comes from Boyd (2004, p.280):

> *In the price-shopping and opinion-shopping turbulence of the 1980s the audit increasingly became a commodity business which had declining margins, and which placed increased stress on the ability of audit firms to maintain a high level of professional integrity independent of those forces.*

Somewhat earlier, Briloff (1990, p.26) had lamented the role of the leaders of the profession for enabling:

> *...those who have an aggressive bent for self-aggrandisement to enter into pursuits which, judged by traditional standards, would be deemed to be incompatible with professional stature - and especially with our much cherished independence ... those in our profession's hierarchy who are presumed to set the standards for excellence ... are principally responsible for the debasement of our professionalism.*

In a comprehensive analysis of the ethical context behind Andersen's deficiencies as Enron's external auditor, Boyd (2004, p.385) argued that unrestrained diversification of the Big Five accounting firms led to multiple catastrophic conflicts of interest.

> *The extent of the big firms' diversification away from the core auditing service was dramatic. Consulting and other non-audit*

> *services comprised just 30 percent of their business in 1976, but grew to be 75 percent of their business twenty-five years later. This shift in product mix must have inevitably meant that the power and dominance of the auditing units within each of the big firms would steadily weaken over these years, while the power of the higher growth consulting units in each firm would correspondingly strengthen.*

It has been argued that the accounting profession's response to the opportunities offered by the changing scope of ambitious businesses in the mid-20th century led to extreme concentration of power and ownership that is unparalleled in any other profession (Boyd, 2004). Further, Wyatt (2003) and Coffee (2002) question whether the current situation of four global accountancy firms is effectively unmanageable from an ethics perspective. Ironically, the growth and structural changes in scope appear to have led to a concurrence of forces contributing to the historically low esteem in which auditors were held (Wyatt, 2003). These included corporate and individual greed, auditors delivering services which impaired independence, becoming too close with clients and participating actively in finding ways to avoid the provisions of accounting standards (Reinstein and McMillan, 2004). Wyatt (2003) argues that the traditional defences to combat these forces no longer work because of the perceived scale of the profession's failure to meet the expectations of investors, creditors and other financial statement users.

Mills and Bettner (1992) discuss the role of ritual in public accounting and the manner in which ritual is used to mask conflicts arising from perceptual gaps concerning the independent auditor's role in society. One of those perceptual gaps is the much discussed expectations gap which refers to differences between perceptions of the large firms and of society generally in regard to the duties and responsibilities of independent auditors (Baker, 1993; Gaa, 1991).

'Fairness of disclosure' has been used to characterise the expectations gap, where a difference exists between what the public and accounting professionals perceive as constituting fair disclosure (Ruland and Lindblom, 1992). The public expects more of accountants in terms of insuring against misleading accounts than accountants accept as their duty. Users of accounts expect auditors to 'penetrate into company affairs' (McEnroe and Martens, 2001). The investing public believes the independent audit has a 'public watchdog' function. Attempts by the profession to reduce the expectations gap include:

- clarifying auditors' responsibilities through issuing auditing standards;
- increasing ethical awareness through revisions to codes of professional conduct; and
- efforts to improve ethics education.

Young (1997, p.55) refers to:

> *The failure of auditors to 'educate' the public as to the value of an audit that excluded such tasks [to detect fraud and warn of imminent business failures] from their jurisdictional domain arose from cultural values with which audits were aligned. The public refused to accept that despite credible financial reporting significant fraud could remain undetected and corporations could fail soon after a 'clean' audit report was issued.*

In the mid-1990s, auditors in the US accepted a more direct responsibility for fraud detection in exchange for a reduction in legal exposure in fraud cases (Young, 1997). The profession issued what were referred to as 'expectation gap standards' – SAS Nos 53–61 (Cullinan and Sutton, 2002, p.307). Cullinan and Sutton argue that these standards actually helped the audit firms to develop a re-engineered audit process which de-emphasised direct testing of transactions and balances. Consequently, they facilitated abandoning responsibility for detecting fraudulent financial reporting.

Firm Culture

Models of ethical decision-making commonly recognise that contextual factors such as organisational or professional norms have a significant impact on behaviour in business contexts (Jones *et al.*, 2003; Shafer *et al.*, 2001; Thorne, 1998; Hunt and Vitell, 1991; Trevino, 1986). In the context of accounting firms, previous research has shown that the ethical climate of the firm heavily influences auditors in their ethical reasoning process (Windsor and Ashkanasy, 1995; Ponemon, 1992). Shafer *et al.* (2001, p.274) refer to numerous studies of ethical decision-making in business contexts concluding that one of 'the primary determinants of ethical behaviour is perceptions of what one's peers would do under similar circumstances'. Briloff (1990, p.25) identified as one of the destructive outcomes of the aggressive pursuit of MAS by US public accountancy firms in the 1980s as the 'infusion into the firm's professional environment of the intensely aggressive, competitive proclivities of the MAS cohorts'.

Accounting firms may have high standards and a good reputation, but individuals within the firm may gain personally from behaviour that is inconsistent with high ethical standards, such as giving in to pressure from clients (Fearnley *et al.*, 2002). The effectiveness of the firm's motivational and control structures in steering individual partners towards goals that are congruent with those of the firm may determine the extent of what Fearnley *et al.* describe as this 'free rider' problem.

The effect of changes in firm culture on behaviour within professional accounting firms has been highlighted in the literature (eg. Wyatt, 2003; Zeff, 2003c; Briloff, 1990). The traditional focus of public accounting/auditing firms was on a professionalism that emphasised and displayed trust, honesty and decency. Firms were known to stand up to clients where they disagreed on principle with a particular accounting treatment (Wyatt, 2003; Zeff, 2003b). The policy of being tough on interpreting reporting standards was perceived to be a selling point, a reputation-enhancing characteristic (Wyatt, 2003, p.2). Audit firms were smaller, and leaders and role models were more visible and accessible. Partners in audit firms spoke out forcefully on issues of the day, often without regard to whether clients would find their opinions objectionable. Professional behaviour was more explicitly developed through apprenticeships, and pre-requisites for promotion to be qualified accountants. In the final thirty or forty years of the 20th century, the culture changed to promoting revenue growth and profitability as the firms' most important objectives, and to a situation where to risk losing clients for matters of accounting principle was considered naïve (Wyatt, 2003). For example, Wyatt (2003, p.2) believes that audit firms' services were expanded in the last three decades of the 20th century to the point where 'almost any service that could generate revenue was undertaken'. Singleton-Green (2002, p.23) referred to a comment made in the early 1990s by Sir Bryan Carsberg, then Secretary-General of the International Accounting Standards Committee, that it wouldn't surprise him if one of the large accountancy firms had decided to branch out into cleaning windows! According to Wyatt, the following phenomena contributed to the changed culture:

- new personnel hired by accounting firms, often into senior positions, lacked a background in professional accounting and the traditional values associated with that background;
- rapidly growing consulting arms from the 1970s, that were increasingly more valued by the firms with those professionals receiving higher compensation than audit or tax;
- audit and tax partners increasingly being pressurised to generate increased revenues and profits;

- advancement within the firms and the ability to sell additional services were increasingly correlated;
- these more aggressive commercially-minded role models for advancement were highly visible and influenced the value systems of professionals starting out in their careers;
- those with substantial technical skills were increasingly undermined, and relatively sidelined; and
- a greed culture infiltrated audit firms in much the same way as it infiltrated other aspects of late 20th century capitalist economies.

The climate within large firms was considered incompatible with the belief that a partner could, or should, stand up to clients, and partners faced sanctions, including dismissal from the firm, if they did not achieve their targets (Zeff, 2003c).

The effect of the late 1990s trend towards corporate ownership of American CPA firms had the effect of desensitising CPAs to traditional professional values (Shafer *et al.*, 2002). Shafer *et al.* (2002) argue that this change in ownership structure posed potential threats to the independence and ethical standards of public accounting firms. In the context of global accounting firms, previous research also suggests that cross-cultural differences can cause differences in interpretations of ethical issues addressed in ethical codes (Karnes *et al.*, 1990) and in auditors' responses to ethical dilemmas (Arnold *et al.*, 1999; Cohen *et al.*, 1995; 1993).

Ethical challenges

In the context of legitimate expectations of accountancy firms in their role as State-mandated external auditors, and based on public and official rhetoric from the accountancy profession, reservations have been expressed in the business and professional press (see, eg. Brown and Dugan, 2002; Dugan, 2002; Dunn and Stewart, 1999; Bruce, 1996) and elsewhere about the ethical standards of accountancy firms. The major areas of ethical concern investigated, critiqued and analysed in the literature, and reviewed in this section of the report, include the existence and impact of conflicts of interest on professional behaviour, auditor independence and audit quality. In addition, the advocacy role played by accountancy firms for client management positions and their association with earnings management and with other questionable financial activities is discussed in the context of the ethics of accountancy firms.

As noted by Fischer and Rosenzweig (1995, p.434):

> *Accountants perform the crucial function of preparing organisational statements which are fair representations of the organisation's financial status; they are in effect gatekeepers of the public trust in our institutions. Therefore, it is crucially important that members of the accounting profession have a reputation of solid integrity, and that this reputation be deserved.*

Conflicts of interest

> *In a pluralistic society, not one but many expectations must be met. Therefore, resolution of what is right to do produces a balance of obligations and satisfactions. Ideally full satisfaction of the expectations of all parties would constitute the most ethical behaviour. This is impossible, for expectations are often contradictory and sometimes exceed social sanction* (Bartels, 1967, cited in Finn *et al.*, 1988, p.606).

At their most basic conceptualisation, ethical problems can arise when individuals interact with other people (Finn *et al.*, 1988). Conflict is viewed by Mills and Bettner (1992, p.186) as:

> *A dynamic social process, characterised by an environment wherein members subscribe and react to incompatible cognitions, beliefs, values and goals.*

Other definitions from the literature explain and illustrate the nature of ethical conflict as follows:

> *Ethical conflict occurs when people perceive that their duties toward one group are inconsistent with their duties and responsibilities toward some other group (including one's self)* (Finn *et al.*, 1988, p.606).

> *'Conflict of interest' refers specifically to situations where one owes a duty to one party but other interests exist which may interfere with the observation of that duty* (Gaa, 1994, p.97).

> *... a situation in which a person has a private or personal interest sufficient to appear to influence the objective exercise of his or her official duties as, say, a public official, an employee, or a professional* (MacDonald *et al.*, 2002, p.68).

The confusion that exists within public practice of accounting regarding the identity of 'the client' reflects the classic conflict of interest problem for auditors. Mayhew and Pike (2004, p.799) describe the problem as 'a lack of clarity about for whom the audit firm truly works'. Jones *et al.* (2003, p.45) refer to external auditors' 'unique role in being obligated to the shareholders despite their close relationship with management'. This leads to ethical dilemmas for external auditors that are different from those confronted by accountants in industry or internal auditors. Audit firms have been increasingly criticised for focusing on pleasing client management to the detriment of investors (Staubus, 2005; Abdel-khalik, 2002; Benston and Hartgraves, 2002;

Levitt, 2002). Mayhew and Pike provide evidence of such criticisms going back to the mid-1950s.

A possible conflict of interest has been inferred in empirical studies from the relatively high level of non-audit fees received by auditors from their clients (eg. Frankel *et al.*, 2002; Unger, 2001). Counter arguments are sometimes offered that provision of NAS can reduce total audit costs and facilitate better quality audits due to better knowledge of the client business. Substantial research also investigates the implications of audit firms providing non-audit services to their audit clients. By providing these services, auditors leave themselves open to criticism of compromising their objectivity, independence and prioritisation of the public interest (Canning and Gwilliam, 1999). A comprehensive analysis of conflicts of interests between auditing and consulting is provided in Boyd (2004).

Many research studies have sought to produce evidence of a conflict of interest between audit and consulting work provided for the same client, but these have generally been inconclusive (Crasswell *et al.*, 2002; Kleinman *et al.*, 1998). Some research has not supported the contention that high non-audit service fees suggest a conflict of interest for auditors (eg. Ashbaugh *et al.*, 2003; DeFond *et al.*, 2002), while others have supported this hypothesis in certain circumstances (see, eg. Sharma and Sidhu, 2001). Conflicts of interest from independence violations are discussed in greater detail in the next sub-section.

Conflicts of interest are morally harmful in that they corrode trust (MacDonald *et al.*, 2002) and trust is the lifeblood of the accountancy profession. Perceptions of conflicts of interest also erode stakeholder trust, even when the individual at the centre of the perceived conflict 'is in fact of unflinching integrity.' Mills and Bettner (1992, p.185) note 'that accounting and auditing are inextricably bound to conflicts through the influence of social and political power'. Hendrickson (1998, p.501) describes the dangers inherent in the auditor-client relationship as follows:

> *...the basic auditor-client relationship creates a direct conflict between auditors' professional responsibilities to investors and the public and their opportunities for personal gain. This conflict, in turn, impairs auditors' ability to be objective, to exercise professional judgement, to tell the truth as they see it, to effectively apply accounting guidelines and principles; and thus, to ensure that the accounting information provided by preparers is relevant and reliable. This impairment also has led regulators to press for standards that require rigid uniformity ... ... which in turn impairs the reliability of the information.*

Auditor independence

> *There is a perception out there – who's to say it is not a reality that auditors are too close to management, the very ones on whom they are supposed to be reporting. All we need is a couple of notorious cases and the public will soon start asking auditors, 'whose side are you on, anyway?'* (Duff, 1988, cited in Neu, 1991, p.307).

According to Ponemon and Gabhart (1990, p.228), the characteristic of 'auditor independence' conveys to the general public 'an image of an auditor having professional integrity, honesty and high moral calibre'. Auditor independence is defined by the Auditing Practices Board as the need to be free from situations and relationships which make it probable that a reasonable and informed third party would conclude that the auditor's objectivity is impaired or could be impaired (APB, 2004). Independence is believed by the APB (APB 2004, ES1, paragraph 12) to underpin objectivity and:

> *...whereas objectivity is a personal behavioural characteristic concerning the auditors' state of mind, independence relates to the circumstances surrounding the audit, including the financial, employment, business and personal relationships between the auditors and their client.*

Auditor independence can be viewed from at least two different perspectives, an economic and a moral viewpoint (Antle, 1999). Antle (p.9) argues that an economic framing of auditor independence is valuable because of 'the favourable effects it has on enhancing the social value of audits'. Society invests in audits for economic reasons. Audits enhance the workings of markets, particularly capital markets (Duska, 2005; Staubus, 2005; Briloff, 2004). Antle (1999, p.9) goes on to say:

> *If auditors' activities create independence problems, economics suggests a cost-benefit test: Do the benefits to society of the auditors' activities outweigh the costs due to impairment of independence? If the benefits outweigh the costs, we are better off with these activities than without them.*

A moral framing of independence sees auditors as professionals, with obligations to the public. Sometimes these obligations require tough decisions to be taken which can be costly to the audit firm. Firms should not engage in activities that appear to impair their effectiveness as professionals, regardless of their incentives (Antle, 1999). Costs and benefits can be argued to be irrelevant when discussing moral issues. However, Antle goes on to argue that the rewards and obligations of auditing are part of the auditors' incentives and that it is a matter of efficiency, rather than vocation, that society demands an element of professional conduct from auditors.

Auditor independence and audit firm ethics are inextricably linked. Historically, the independence of the auditor was one of the cornerstones of the accounting profession's ethos, and certainly today, the profession would claim that its importance has not diminished (APB, 2004). However, the literature suggests that the direction taken by accounting firms in recent decades toward commercialism and competition is incompatible with professionalism, and it questions whether independence, and the integrity and objectivity associated with it, have been abandoned by the 'industry'.

Beattie *et al.* (1999) suggest that independence has two distinct dimensions, independence in fact and independence in appearance, and that both are fundamental to public confidence in financial reporting. Independence in fact is the unbiased mental attitude of the auditor. Independence in appearance is the perception by a reasonable observer that the auditor has no relationship to the audit client that suggests a conflict of interest. Since independence in fact is unobservable, research in the area of auditor independence has focused on identifying factors that influence independence, both positively and negatively, and on assessing their impact upon perceived independence. Factors influencing independence also fall into two categories: economic and regulatory. The primary economic factor is the provision of NAS to audit clients, and this is complicated by the degree of dependence by the auditor on the audit client and the level of competition in the external audit market. The primary regulatory factor is the degree of laxity of the regulatory framework.

Auditor independence is perceived to be compromised if the auditor is economically dependent on client companies either because the audit is too valuable to lose in its own right, thereby weakening the auditor's ability to stand up to client management in a significant disagreement, or because it is too valuable to lose because of the lost opportunity to provide other services to the client. Fees to audit firms from NAS have been rising more rapidly over time than audit fees (Beattie and Fearnley, 2002). Consequently, concerns are widely expressed that economic dependence leads to compromised auditor objectivity, backbone and integrity. The combination of being potentially too close to client management and too beholding to them for more business has tarnished the perception of external auditors as 'financial detectives' (Revsine, 2002). The flaw in the triangular system of corporate governance (management, auditor and shareholders) that mitigates against a primary focus on providing valid, balanced and honest information to shareholders is very well articulated in Briloff (2004) and in Staubus (2005). The incorrect identification of client company management as 'the client' and, therefore, the one who is to be satisfied by the service provided, exerts pressure on auditor scepticism (Duska, 2005; Briloff, 2004; Gray, 2004; Benston and Hartgraves, 2002).

Abdel-khalik (2002) argues that the threat to auditor independence comes from the institutional arrangements that effectively give management and the Board of Directors control over the appointment and terms of appointment of external auditors, rather than from the same professional firm providing both auditing and consulting services. Abdel-khalik (2002, p.98) state:

> *... [T]hat shareholders elect and appoint the auditor ... is the biggest fallacy in corporate governance today. In today's global economy, corporate ownership is widely dispersed and shareholders, through proxy votes or sheer indifference, have effectively handed over the control of auditor-related decisions (hiring, retention and compensation) to corporate management. The same management will also decide on consulting engagements.'*

In the context of professional firms gearing up to operate at a high level of operating activity, much of which is not repetitive, audit firms are under commercial pressure to maintain and expand business. Thus, the increase in non-audit fees as a proportion of total fee payments to specific firms has exacerbated the traditional debate regarding the impact of MAS and NAS on auditor independence, as noted by Citron (2003, p.250):

> *The growth in multidisciplinary practices, for example, has enabled firms to provide an ever widening range of other services for clients, leading some to argue that their dependency on audit*

> *clients is increasing to unsustainable levels ... In addition, some of the other activities undertaken by accounting firms raise specific independence problems. Thus it has been questioned whether firms' relations with their clients cast doubt over their ability to act as expert witness in court ..., and whether their relationships with banks are compatible with their activities as receivers.*

The provision of NAS by incumbent auditors is a phenomenon which has been intensively debated in recent years by policy-makers, the accountancy profession, practitioners, and academics. The benefits and drawbacks have been contentiously argued. Audit firms make the following arguments in favour of the provision of NAS, as cited by Canning and Gwilliam (1999):

- NAS allow audit firms to diversify, making them less reliant on a single client;
- use of NAS can increase client reliance on the audit firm, lessening the weight and efficacy of the client management threat to change audit firms; and
- NAS give rise to increased auditor knowledge of the client, its systems, and their weaknesses, thereby facilitating a better audit.

Nonetheless, policy-makers and regulators remain sceptical of the benefits and are more convinced by the potentially dysfunctional effects of audit firms providing NAS. For example, audit firms often use the statutory audit as a loss leader to secure more lucrative NAS contracts. They are then potentially compromised by the desire to keep the NAS contracts. The integrity of the audit may be compromised because audit firms are reluctant to confront and antagonise management when contentious audit issues arise. Financial reporting principles developed for US public companies in the wake of the Enron and other financial scandals reflect these concerns by including the following recommendations in relation to audit firms:

> *Audit firms should focus primarily on providing high-quality audit and assurance services and should perform no consulting for audit clients. Audit firm personnel should be selected, evaluated, compensated, and promoted primarily based on technical competence, not on their ability to generate new business. …… …. Audit firms should view public accounting as a noble profession focused on the public interest, not as a competitive business* (Hermanson and Lapides, 2003, p.9).

Independence is perceived to be compromised, even if it is not actually compromised, when the relationship between auditor and client management is too close. In the context of impaired independence of non-executive directors, an American shareholder activist is quoted in Gray (2004, p.M4) as follows: 'There's a natural human impulse to dance with the one who invited you to the party'. The same article went on to quote Warren Buffet, the legendary model of successful investor and analyst, as follows:

> *Too often I was silent when management made proposals that I judged to be counter to the interests of shareholders. In these cases, collegiality trumped independence...*

This is sometimes labelled the familiarity threat (Hussey, 1999) and is only one of the six principal threats to auditors' objectivity identified by APB (2004). The other five are: self-interest threat; self-review threat; management threat; advocacy threat; and intimidation threat. The professional monthly magazine, *Accountancy*, regularly analyses the relationship between FTSE 100 companies' Finance Directors and their auditors (see for example, September issues in 2003 and 2004). This analysis merely confirms the existence of strong links between auditors and client firm management, without drawing any inferences from the facts. Volumes of commentary are on record criticising the relationship between Arthur Andersen and Enron, implying an absence of integrity in the audit (see eg. Brown, 2005; O'Connell, 2004, Reinstein and McMillan, 2004; Copeland, 2003; Lucci, 2003; Dewing and Russell, 2003; Coffee, 2002; Revsine, 2002; Benston and Hartgraves, 2002). The relationship between Elan Pharmaceutical's management and its external auditor was repeatedly highlighted as a factor in the company being discredited in the capital markets during 2002 (Pierce, 2003). Whilst rotation of auditors is sometimes suggested as a safeguard against the familiarity threat, there is no evidence that such a policy is widespread in market economies, although Zeff (2003a) discusses the policy of changing auditors annually and biannually in Du Pont between 1910 and 1954. Despite limited documentation to explain the Du Pont founder's policy on rotation of auditor, Zeff (p.13) concludes from the available evidence that Mr du Pont was concerned to 'prevent or expose any collusion among officers, and even the external auditor was not above suspicion'.

It is argued that the changing structure of the accounting profession in the 1970s and 1980s, whereby major accounting firms began to employ many more trainees than they historically needed to replace retirees and to accommodate growth, fuelled the diminution of auditor independence (Boyd, 2004, p.382). Boyd's argument is that 'the shedding of the newly excessive numbers of articling students to clients' produced a win-win situation for all concerned. There was a high probability of future business relationships with 'biased clients'. This strategy in the context of the US Andersen firm was described by Toffler (2003, p.25) as follows:

> *They all knew that their chances of making partner were slim, and that they were in for a rigorous, exhausting few years as the 'grunts'.*

> *But there was that big fat brass ring at the end. Even if they didn't make partner, the opportunities for an Arthur Andersen-trained accountant were many and choice. We would 'tell them that they should find other employment because their future was limited,' said Spacek in an oral history, 'but ... help them get into good jobs because they were what I call our 'fifth column'. When they got into the business, they remembered their alma mater, that's all.' The point was to maintain goodwill, so that even the people who didn't make it remembered their experience fondly and would go out of their way to steer business to the good old firm.*

Boyd (2004, p.382) acknowledges there has been a recent culture shift towards identifying a potential ethical problem with this strategy, particularly where it involves transfers of senior audit firm staff:

> *The ethics of this strategy of the big accounting firms encouraging former audit team members to transfer to employment within the organisations that they were continuing to audit did not appear to be a matter for widespread concern in the immediate period leading up to the Enron scandal.*

Empirical evidence of link between NAS and impaired independence

As previously noted, academic research has distinguished between independence in fact and independence in appearance. Empirical research, conducted to establish whether the provision of NAS actually compromises auditor independence, has failed to offer persuasive evidence one way or the other (see Reynolds *et al.*, 2004). Although most empirical research to date has concluded that independence is not impaired, this research suffers from the limitations of the research method used. Because independence cannot be measured directly, several proxies have been used as a surrogate for independence. Indirect research on

NAS and independence involves using phenomena such as earnings management, financial statement restatements, and qualified audit opinions as proxies for impaired auditor independence. For example, Frankel *et al.* (2002) investigated whether auditor independence affected the quality of reported earnings. They conducted an empirical analysis of discretionary accruals and fee ratios (audit fees, non-audit fees, and total fees) and found significant association between the level of non-audit fees and the level of discretionary accruals (suggesting impaired earnings quality). Ashbaugh *et al.* (2003) conducted a similar empirical study, but they used a slightly adjusted measure of discretionary accruals. Ashbaugh *et al.* (2003) refuted the findings of Frankel *et al.* (2002). Similarly, Chung and Kallapur (2003) examined whether there was an association between discretionary accruals and client importance (as measured by the ratio of the client's audit and non-audit fees to the audit firm's overall US revenues). They concluded that there was no association, thus again casting doubt on the empirical evidence that NAS compromised auditor independence. Using yet another measure of earnings quality, Raghunandan *et al.* (2003) investigated whether there was an association between those companies that restated their financial statements and non-audit fees received by the incumbent auditor at the time of, and prior to, the restatement. Again, they found no association between the likelihood of restatement and the levels of non-audit fees.

DeFond *et al.* (2002) suggested that the indirect approach being adopted in earlier studies was imprecise and ineffective for two reasons. First, the use of discretionary accruals as a proxy for earnings management is problematic and inaccurate, as demonstrated when Ashbaugh *et al.* (2003) refuted the findings of Frankel *et al.* (2002) by using a different measure of discretionary accruals. Secondly, the use of earnings management as an indicator of impaired auditor judgement introduces noise into the results, because auditors have not been proven to have strong influence on the quality of client earnings. In response to these problems, DeFond *et al.* (2002) suggested that using the audit report, and the opinion contained therein, in independence studies would be more effective because the audit opinion was controlled by the auditor, and measuring the audit opinion was relatively straightforward. They then tested whether the provision of NAS impaired auditor independence by using auditors' tendency to issue a going concern audit opinion as a proxy for auditor independence. Their results suggested that the provision of NAS did not impair auditor independence.

However, research on the perception of independence in the light of the provision of NAS tells a different story. There appears to be agreement both among practitioners and audit clients that the purchase of NAS from the auditor gives an impression of impropriety. Firth (1997) examined whether clients, who had high, or potentially high, agency costs and a greater need for the appearance of independence, purchased relatively smaller amounts of NAS. The results indicated that such companies purchased less NAS from the incumbent audit firm, suggesting that the agency cost of the appearance of using a compromised audit firm was too high. Canning and Gwilliam (1999) investigated the effects of the provision of NAS on perceptions of auditor independence. Auditor independence was perceived as significantly diminished where personnel involved in the audit, rather than a separate department, provided NAS to clients. Reinstein and McMillan (2004) provided circumstantial evidence from the prior literature of situations where independence was perceived to be impaired:

- where audit fees were used as loss leaders;
- where large firms boosted profits by focusing on NAS (often to cover prior audit failure settlement fines);
- where Big 5 firms earned more in non-audit fees than in audit fees for specified years; and
- in the context of Enron, sharp practices within partner ranks was asserted in financial media and enormous pressure was reported to have been exerted on Andersen partners to generate fee income.

These studies suggest that even if it cannot be proved conclusively that the provision of NAS actually impairs auditor independence, there is certainly a strong perception that it does, and that appears to be sufficient justification for some practitioners and companies to avoid the practice, and for policy-makers and regulators to condemn the practice.

Audit Quality

Audit Quality has been defined by Chaney *et al.* (2003, p.488) as:

> *… the likelihood of issuing the correct opinion on the financial statements of a given client. Audit quality is assumed to be the function of two specific auditor attributes: competence, or the likelihood of discovering a violation, if one exists; and independence, or the likelihood of reporting truthfully if a breach is discovered.*

Quality is a complex social construct which is not easily observable by either regulators or the general public (Sikka, 2004). Lee (1994) discusses how auditors are caught in a dilemma where improved definition/articulation of their 'quality labels' might enhance their claims to professionalism on the one hand, but expose the body of knowledge to greater external inspection, on the other. Quality labels include terminology such as 'true and fair view' as used in Europe and 'present fairly' as used in US. Lee (1994, p.43) argues that these labels 'describe the overriding quality standard for the content of published financial statements'. A stated purpose of monitoring audit firms is to enable a regulator to satisfy itself that auditors have complied with regulations, as distinct from setting out to ensure that a good quality audit is done (Fuerman, 2004).

The literature provides some indirect evidence of audit quality reduction as a response to the commercial pressures experienced in recent decades (Boyd, 2004; Pierce and Sweeney, 2004; Brown, 2002; Willett and Page, 1996). For example, the number of audit failures has increased, and litigation against audit firms, with resultant increases in professional indemnity insurance premiums, has also occurred (Boyd, 2004). Auditors have also been criticised for issuing clean audit reports in situations where companies have gone into liquidation or receivership soon afterwards (Brown, 2005; Bryan-Low, 2002).

A substantial literature based on questionnaire evidence investigates the impact on audit quality of time pressure in audit firms where doubtful audit evidence is being passed over by audit teams under time pressure to complete assignments, such as the failure to test the required number of items in a sample, or falsifying working-papers (Sikka, 2004; Willett and Page, 1996). Research into the complexities of audit firms' management control systems has gained momentum over the last twenty years, focusing in particular on the effects of time pressure on the behaviour of individual auditors and ultimately on audit quality. A direct association between the behavioural consequences of time pressure and audit firm ethical standards is rarely, if ever addressed in the literature. However, the literature suggests a tacit knowledge by the firms that this behaviour exists among audit staff (Pierce and Sweeney, 2003; Otley and Pierce, 1996b; Willet and Page, 1996).

The presence of severe time pressures in the auditor's work environment was first highlighted in findings from a major US survey (Rhode, 1978) and was deemed to arise from a combination of circumstances. Time budgets were used to control the costs incurred on audit assignments, these budgets were seen by audit staff as being very tight and sometimes unattainable. However, successfully meeting budget and avoiding over-runs was seen by auditors as being critically important for achieving good personal performance evaluation ratings and progressing within the firm. Consistently high levels of time pressures were subsequently reported in a wide range of studies in the US (eg. Malone and Roberts, 1996; Kelley and Margheim, 1987; Alderman and Deitrick, 1982), the

UK (Willett and Page, 1996), New Zealand (Cook and Kelley, 1991) and Ireland (Pierce and Sweeney, 2003; Otley and Pierce, 1996a). While the predominant form of time pressure has continued to be that associated with time budgets, more recent research has distinguished between time budgets, leading to chronic time pressure (persistent, relatively unchanging), and time deadlines, leading to more acute and potentially more damaging time pressure (short-term, high intensity impact) (DeZoort and Lord, 1997).

The consequences of this time pressure, in terms of individual auditors' response behaviours, have also been examined. Consistent with the general literature on management control systems, this research has reported evidence of a positive correlation between the intensity of time pressure and reported levels of dysfunctional behaviour (eg. Dalton and Kelley, 1997; Malone and Roberts, 1996; Otley and Pierce, 1996b; Kelley and Margheim, 1990). The most serious of these behaviours are potentially damaging to audit quality and have been described in the literature as audit quality reduction behaviour (Alderman and Deitrick, 1982), or quality threatening behaviour (Sweeney and Pierce, 2004; Pierce and Sweeney, 2003). This includes any behaviour by auditors that has the potential to adversely affect audit quality, such as prematurely signing off tests without completing all the work or noting the omission, biasing sample selection and making unauthorised reductions in sample sizes. One particular form of behaviour that has been found to be prevalent is the tendency of some auditors to under-state the number of hours worked on a particular client in order to avoid budget over-runs (Anderson-Gough *et al.*, 2001; Otley and Pierce, 1996a; McNair, 1991; Dirsmith and Covaleski, 1985). Usually referred to as under-reporting of time (URT), there are conflicting opinions in the literature as to whether this is functional or dysfunctional behaviour, since it could be interpreted as a sign of organisational commitment, but it appears to be explicitly requested by some members of senior management and tacitly approved by others, as it does not have a direct impact on audit quality (Anderson-Gough *et al.*, 2001; McNair, 1991). However, there is consistent evidence that URT is contrary to firm policies, and it has been associated with negative personal feelings and the perpetuation of unrealistically tight budgets, leading to the possible incidence of quality threatening behaviour in later periods (Pierce and Sweeney, 2003; Otley and Pierce, 1996b).

The research method used for most of these studies was anonymous surveys of audit staff, underlining the extremely sensitive nature of the subject matter, while a small number of studies have used an experimental case approach (eg. McDaniel, 1990; Margheim & Pany, 1986) and interviews (Herrbach, 2002). While the methods used in any particular study are necessarily limited, the high degree of consistency in the findings provides credible evidence of relatively high levels of dysfunctional behaviour and a positive association between the incidence of this behaviour and the intensity of time pressure. Most of the research has focused on audit seniors because this has been regarded as the most pressurised position in the firm (Kelley and Seiler, 1982), although the issue of dysfunctional behaviour at partner level has also been addressed in the literature (Carcello *et al.*, 1996; Miller, 1992).

These issues regarding the incidence of potentially damaging behaviours in response to cost control procedures have been discussed in the context of a cost-quality conflict (McNair, 1991). Whereas costs, represented mainly by professional hours, are highly visible and amenable to precise measurement, audit quality is more difficult to measure. Not only do clients experience difficulty in assessing audit quality, auditors themselves have difficulty in judging whether or not they have conducted a 'good' audit (Power, 2003). In an investigation of auditor and client management decision-making processes in UK listed companies, Beattie *et al.* (2004, p.16) identified poor relationships between the audit partner (AEP) and the finance director (FD) as a contributory factor to 'low quality outcomes' of negotiations on important audit issues. A contributory factor to the poor relationship was identified as:

> *...where the FD has previously been in a position senior to the AEP in the same audit firm (which appears to put the AEP at a disadvantage) or where there is a significant age and experience gap between them.*

Implications for audit firms' management control systems are set out in the work of Abernethy and Stoelwinder (1995), who advocated the use of 'less obtrusive forms' of management control for activities that were less amenable to traditional forms of control, such as the provision of professional services. Personnel, social, clan and self controls could be described as less obtrusive forms of control, whereas output, input and behavioural controls were seen as traditional forms of control. Abernethy and Stoelwinder (1995) suggested that for complex work processes, it might be appropriate to rely more on 'professional' control and that if an organisation imposed tight bureaucratic controls in the work environment of professionals that served to curb their autonomy, a conflict was likely to arise. In situations where professional training took place in an organisation such as the accountancy profession, the level of professional autonomy desired might differ considerably from the level encouraged by the organisation. Abernethy and Stoelwinder pointed out that an organisation needed to supplement the social and self controls of the professional with training and socialisation strategies to ensure that there was congruence between the goals of the organisation and those of the professional.

A poor audit does not cause failure (Hamilton, 2004). However, with a poor audit, people can disguise the reality of what is going on. Arguments in the literature focus on how the contemporary approach to auditing has allowed problems to persist. It is argued that corners are cut, junior or cheap staff are used, and excessive reliance is placed on poorly understood, and sometimes incorrectly applied, statistical techniques. Sikka (2004) argues that audit failures are a product of the deficient values governing audit firms. However, he laments the difficulty experienced by researchers in gaining 'access to client data or live assignments to enable researchers to study their organisational life' (p.187).

Lobbying

> *More and more it became clear that audit firms did not want to do anything to rock the boat with clients, potentially jeopardising their chief source of income. Consulting contracts were turning accounting firms into extensions of management – even cheerleaders at times* (Levitt, 2002, cited in Boyd, 2004, p.386).

Lobbying by vested interests or concerned parties is common throughout democratic societies. An extensive literature on lobbying in accounting contexts exists. Accountancy bodies and firms lobby on behalf of clients (eg. on financial reporting issues) and for self-interest (eg. to maintain statutory audit or self-regulation etc.). The extent to which any of this lobbying behaviour is ethical or not has rarely been addressed in the prior research, although the role of auditors as advocates for their client interests has been criticised (Zeff, 2003b; Levitt, 2002).

Lobbying on accounting issues is the collective term for the action taken by interested parties to influence the rule-making and accounting standard-setting bodies (Sutton, 1984). Newman (1981) examined the power over standards exercised by the large accounting firms, the then 'Big 8', and found that the power held by Big 8 firms was greater than their proportional representation on the UK Auditing Practices Board and the Financial Accounting Standards Board (FASB). A similar conclusion was drawn by Boyd (2004) with regard to Big Firm influence on professional body strategies, activities and policies.

Dwyer and Roberts (2004) detail how in the early-1990s, the AICPA and the Big 5 accounting firms actively participated in constitutional politics to directly lobby and support congressional candidates who were in positions to affect the content of legislation that related to the profession, such that subsequently, when the FASB was pressured by congress or the senate, the pressure was in reality stemming from the AICPA, which was largely controlled by the large accounting firms. They also found, in an analysis of the political campaign contributions made to legislators, that the US profession showed a preference for legislators who were sympathetic to pro-business agendas. Similarly, legislators who received financial support from the profession tended to favour conservative agendas and tended to oppose agendas advanced by civil rights, labour, liberal, and women's groups.

Zeff (2002) details numerous instances internationally where proposed changes to accounting rules were undermined by lobbying from political, industrial, and professional quarters. In 1992, the IASC was poised to eliminate the use of LIFO, and despite opposition by the International Organisation of Securities Commissions, the US and Canada (where LIFO was permitted) supported the proposal. However, unexpectedly, it was defeated when delegations from Korea, Italy, Germany and Japan voted against it. It appeared the delegations were put under pressure by companies operating in these countries, where LIFO was allowable under income tax rules, and the financial reporting rules were linked to the tax rules. A similar situation occurred when the Accounting Standards Committee (ASC) reversed their position on accounting for deferred tax in the mid-1970s, succumbing to pressure from the UK Government, clearing banks and big industry. Many of the submissions made by clearing banks and industry were submitted by accounting firms on behalf of their clients. Furthermore, McKee *et al.* (1991) provide evidence that accounting firms supported the positions of their clients when lobbying the FASB in relation to accounting for software costs and they concluded that the firms were acting as advocates for their clients which they opined was potentially detrimental to the intellectual honesty of the standard-setting process.

Zeff (2002) described similar situations in the US where, despite support for the FASB by the powerful SEC, the FASB, on three separate occasions in the 1990s, ceded to pressure from various lobbying parties. During the period 1990-1993, the American Bankers Association, aided by the chairman of the Federal Reserve Board and the chairman of the Federal Deposit Insurance Corporation, lobbied to prevent the FASB requiring that all marketable securities be shown at fair value and that changes year-on-year in those values be included in earnings. A diluted proposal was subsequently passed, requiring changes to be set against shareholders' equity.

In the period 1992-1995, there was severe opposition to a FASB exposure draft which required companies using stock options as a means of compensation to estimate the fair value of the options and charge the expense against income. This time, pressure came primarily from the Senate, because, as indicated by Dwyer and Roberts (2004), the AICPA and large accounting firms had significant influence over congressmen and senators. Eventually, congressional pressure became so intense that the SEC chairman feared that approval of the FASB proposal would jeopardise private sector control of accounting standard-setting. The eventual regulation was to disclose in a footnote the estimated dilutive effect of stock options on reported earnings. Further, Hill *et al.* (2002) found that the higher the level of stock-based compensation within a firm, the less likely that firm was to favour recording the expense, supporting the hypothesis that the lobbying was motivated by economic self-interest.

Finally, Zeff (2002) describes the period 1996-2001, when industry and the profession lobbied strongly, through congress, to prevent new regulations on accounting for business combinations and to introduce the mandatory amortisation of goodwill. Lobbyists were particularly opposed to the proposed mandatory amortisation of goodwill. The result of the lobbying was that instead of mandatory amortisation, only periodic impairment testing was required.

Puro (1985) examined the findings of the Metcalf Report, which alleged that the big accounting firms, the then Big 8, had, by virtue of large financial contributions and Board representations, more influence in the standard-setting process than other participants, and in that way determined how the rules would be written. Metcalf further alleged that the Big 8 acted to disadvantage smaller firms, and that where they lobbied, they acted in their client's interests, rather than in the public interest. Puro did not find significant empirical evidence to support these claims. While he found that the big firms participated more in the process, this could not be inferred as dominance, since smaller firms might not have participated because they might have felt they had no interests at stake, or, they might have felt that their interests were already represented by participating firms. In addition, Puro found little evidence that the big firms acted as a bloc. He actually found as many instances where big firms disagreed as when they agreed. It was also found that the opinions of the big firms were not consistently out of step with other representatives of industry. Puro also found little evidence to support the claim that the big firms' wishes prevailed over smaller firms in the standard-setting process. It was inferred from submissions to the standard-setting process, however, that the level of disagreement among big firms meant that they were in fact acting on behalf of their clients and not in the public interest, and that the disagreement reflected disagreement among various businesses and clients.

Gilfedder and Ó hÓgartaigh (1998) found that preparers of financial statements, specifically large accounting firms, dominated the standard-setting process in the UK (the ASB), in contrast to users who did not participate to any great extent. Sikka and Willmott (1995) examined responses to the proposed 8th EU Directive. At the time, Coopers and Lybrand publicly urged all their clients to lobby the UK government on the proposal to curb the sale of non-audit services. The lobby was successful, and the Directive was enacted without any of the changes proposed by the UK government.

Earnings Management

> *The tangled web that is woven when creative accounting is practiced as a critical aspect of management and accountability* (Briloff, 1990, p.25).

The professional image of accountants is questioned when the integrity of financial statements is undermined. Such questioning has occurred in the context of overstated company earnings and massaged financial condition, falsification of corporate records, lying, cover-ups, improperly applied accounting principles and false disclosures (Reinstein and McMillan, 2004; Finn *et al.*, 1988). Capital markets provide companies with both positive and negative incentives to manage earnings (Clikeman *et al.*, 2001a; Dechow and Skinner, 2000; Revsine, 1991). Substantial contract and economic incentives exist to 'motivate selective financial misrepresentation' (Revsine, 2002). These include:

- increasing reported profits to avoid debt covenant violations;
- under-reporting company earnings so that favourable prices in management buyouts can be facilitated;
- managing reported earnings upwards so that bonus compensation can be increased; and
- managing earnings 'appropriately' so that loans can be obtained on more favourable terms, the company's share price can be protected or supported and smoothing year-to-year revenues so that earnings growth can be reported.

Despite the potential of well-developed accounting and disclosure practices to serve capital markets well, Briloff (2004, p.791) describes contemporary responses to capital market pressures, such as preparers of financial reports generating spurious popular financial metrics as follows:

> *... GAAP, if applied with integrity and effectively disciplined by ... GAAS could provide the frame of reference for meaningful financial statement analysis .... Regrettably that kind of disciplined approach could not produce the irrationally exuberant numbers demanded by those who were expecting ecstasy from NASDAQ. ... ... they developed such notions as 'EBITDA' (earnings before interest, taxes, depreciation and amortisation), 'FFO' (funds from operations), and 'Pro Forma Earnings' (whatever number you have in mind).*

Non-GAAP earnings' measures are generally perceived to undermine earnings quality. Impaired earnings quality has been defined as 'the extent to which net income reported on the income statement differs from 'true' (unbiased and accurate) earnings' (Hodge, 2003, p.37). In an empirical study which investigated the perceptions of relatively sophisticated investors, Hodge (2003) concluded that perceived earnings quality for all publicly traded firms had declined over time, as had perceived auditor independence and the perceived reliability of audited financial information. Widespread concerns about earnings management contributed to these adverse perceptions.

Healy and Wahlen (1999) suggest that earnings management occurs when managers use judgement in financial reporting and in structuring financial transactions to alter financial reports, either to mislead some shareholders about the underlying economic performance of the company, or to influence contractual outcomes that depend on reported accounting numbers. Earnings management has been defined in a number of different ways, including the following:

> *Any action on the part of management which affects reported income and which provides no true economic advantage to the organization and may, in fact, in the long-term, be detrimental* (Merchant and Rockness, 1994, p.79).

> *... a purposeful intervention in the external financial reporting process, with the intent of obtaining some private gain (as opposed to say, merely facilitating the neutral operation of the process)...* (Schipper, 1989, p.92).

The definition provided by Elias (2002, p.34) identifies both intention and consequence as necessary features:

> *... actions by division managers which serve to increase (decrease) current reported earnings of a division without a corresponding increase (decrease) in the long-term economic profitability of this division.*

Whilst that provided by Gaa (2004, p.351) focuses on the selfish motivation behind earnings management:

> *...strategic behavior, involving the manipulation of financial statements for one's own advantage.*

Referring to prior literature, Nelson *et al.* (2002, p.176) define earnings management as:

> *...non-neutral financial reporting in which managers intervene intentionally in the financial reporting process to produce some private gain (Schipper 1989). Managers can intervene by modifying how they interpret financial accounting standards and accounting data, or by timing or structuring transactions (Healy and Wahlen 1999). Because many such interventions are difficult to distinguish from appropriate applications of GAAP, the definition of earnings management hinges fundamentally on managerial intent, which is difficult to assess using ex post accounting information* (Dechow and Skinner, 2000).

It has been suggested that the term earnings management is too polite a description for what is in effect 'cooking the books' and often financial statement fraud. Earnings management activities can mislead financial statement users and sometimes are precursors of more serious activities such as fraudulent activities (Loomis, 1999). Dechow and Skinner (2000) provide a useful analysis of the distinction between earnings management and fraud. See also Nieschwietz *et al.* (2000) for a review of empirical research on external auditors' detection of financial statement fraud, and Rezaee (2005) for a discussion of causes, consequences and deterrence of financial statement fraud. Earnings management was identified as the most important ethical issue facing the accounting profession long before the Andersen implosion, not only because of the immediate consequences for the affected parties, but also because of the erosion of trust between shareholders and companies (Clikeman *et al.*, 2001a; Levitt, 1998; Merchant and Rockness, 1994).

There has been a substantial amount of research investigating earnings management. Nelson *et al.* (2002) classify this research into studies which infer earnings management (EM), ie. 'unexpected accruals' studies where EM is inferred when accruals differ from expectations in the direction favoured by the incentive proxy and 'distributional' studies which test whether earnings' distributions around benchmarks differ in some predicted way from what would be expected in the absence of earnings management. Other studies focus on analysing disciplinary outcomes (eg. 'enforcement-release' studies) for insights or on auditors' decisions when faced with potential EM ('adjusting-entry' studies). Experimental studies examine earnings management related decisions made in laboratory settings. See Dechow and Skinner (2000) for a good explanation and Dye (1988) for an examination of EM incentives from a shareholder perspective. In particular, research examines whether or not earnings management exists (DeGeorge *et al.*, 1999; Burgstahler and Eames, 1998; Burgstahler and Dichev, 1997; Burgstahler, 1997), incentives for earnings management (Anderson *et al.*, 2004; Baker *et al.*, 2003; Latham and Jacobs, 2000; Dye, 1988), and its relative magnitude and consequences for capital markets (Healy and Wahlen, 1999). However, few studies have examined the ethical perceptions of earnings management activity (Elias, 2002).

Dye (1988) developed a model to identify situations in which certain users of financial statements benefited from earnings management. Focusing on two classes of user, shareholders and non-shareholders, his model indicated that shareholders had a demand for earnings management that boosted the share price in the short run, whereas non-shareholders did not. While managers engaged in earnings management to increase the stock price, they also engaged in earnings management for personal gain. Kaplan (2001) refers to the former as 'company intent' and the latter as 'individual intent'. He acknowledges that where the intent of earnings management is personal gain by managers, shareholders would not benefit and, therefore, would not have a demand for certain types of earnings management.

A key driver of aggressive accounting, in a study of audit partners and finance directors of UK listed companies, was found to be financial difficulty, and particularly the need to stay within debt covenants (Beattie *et al.*, 2004). Beattie *et al.* concluded that financial reporting quality could change rapidly as a company's circumstances changed (eg. a decline in profitability or the expectation of a hostile bid). Gillett and Uddin (2005, p.73) found that company size emerged as 'a potentially important red flag in detecting fraudulent financial reporting' in their examination of CFO intentions for fraudulent financial reporting based on the self-reported intentions of 139 CFOs. Contrary to expectations, they concluded that the compensation structure did not affect their intentions, although they acknowledged that 'more research is required on the measurement of compensation structure and on its effect on willingness to commit financial statement fraud' (p.73).

Two types of earnings management manipulation were identified in the literature: operating manipulations and accounting manipulations (Elias, 2002; Grant *et al.*, 2000; Fischer and Rosenzweig, 1995; Bruns and Merchant, 1990). Operating manipulations occur when operating decisions affect cash flow and net income for a period, eg. easing credit terms to increase sales. Accounting manipulations arise when the flexibility in accounting standards is used to alter accounting numbers (Elias, 2002). Rather than ensuring that financial reports reflect an enterprise's underlying performance, accounting manipulations are used to reflect the desires of management in order to meet capital market expectations (Grant *et al.*, 2000). Nelson *et al.* (2002) identified the occurrence of earnings management in numerous accounting areas based on questionnaires completed by 253 audit managers and partners from one 'Big 5 firm' which identified 515 specific experiences of attempted earnings management by client companies. The responding auditors believed that earnings management was motivated by a variety of incentives, including:

> *The need to meet analysts' estimates and influence the stock market, to reach targets set by compensation contracts or debt covenants, to communicate economic information to stakeholders, and to smooth income or improve future income, as well as by combinations of these incentives* (Nelson *et al.*, 2002, p.176).

Public and regulator perceptions of inadequate audits have increased dramatically in the wake of the recent financial scandals. Many commentators have suggested that the commercial focus of prioritising client management satisfaction over professional reputation has led to compromised auditor integrity. They ask 'where were the auditors?' and they question whether professional ethics have any meaning in the 'accounting industry'. Perceived problems with earnings management are that it obscures facts that investors and lenders ought to know, thus leaving them ignorant of the true value or stability of the business

(Elias, 2002; Clikeman *et al.*, 2001a), and it can have negative social consequences, especially in resource allocation among stakeholders (Healy and Wahlen, 1999). Earnings management causes trust between shareholders and companies to erode (Levitt, 1998). A counter argument is that current shareholders encourage earnings management in order to maximise the value of their shareholdings at the expense of future shareholders, thereby creating a managerial incentive to manage earnings. Schipper (1989) accepted that earnings management was inherent in the financial reporting system and argued that this did not eliminate the usefulness of accounting earnings. Parfet (2000) also argues that earnings management is not necessarily a bad thing. He believes that managers should use all available options to increase shareholders' wealth, including 'good' earnings management.

Empirical evidence of earnings management

Although empirical research confirmed for some time the existence of earnings management, evidence on the frequency and magnitude of earnings management throughout the 1990s was sparse, as was evidence of how earnings were managed (Healy and Wahlen, 1999). While anecdotal evidence and instinct led regulators to accuse managers, accountants and the wider business community of engaging in earnings management, the profession relied to some extent on the fact that academic evidence failed conclusively to address many of the issues surrounding earnings management or its consequences and ethicality (Merchant and Rockness, 1994). Kaplan (2001) also refers to the paucity of research on the ethicalness of earnings management.

Empirical research has offered circumstantial evidence that earnings management occurs. Burgstahler and Dichev (1997), Burgstahler (1997) and DeGeorge *et al.* (1999) report that small reported losses are unusually rare, while small reported profits are unusually common. Earnings management is often driven by the perceived imperative of meeting capital market expectations (Loomis, 1999). Brown (1998), Burgstahler and Eames (1998) and DeGeorge *et al.* (1999) report an unusually large number of zero and small positive analyst forecast errors, and conversely, an unusually small number of negative analyst forecast errors. This trend is reported to be more pronounced in growth stocks. This evidence substantiates the claim that companies are responding to a 'meet or beat' pressure imposed by the market (ie. that a failure to at least meet analysts' forecasted performance will result in a disproportionate fall in stock prices). Dechow et al. (1996) investigated motivations for earnings management and identified characteristics of firms that manipulated earnings and negative consequences for their cost of capital subsequent to the manipulation being made public.

However, there is disagreement among academics relating to the effect of earnings management, such as whether earnings management affects resource allocation, ie. whether investors see through it or not. For example, Teoh, Welsh and Wong (1998) and Teoh, Wong and Rao (1998) find that firms with income-increasing abnormal accruals in the year of a seasoned equity issue or initial public offering suffer significant stock underperformance subsequent to the offerings. This demonstrates that investors' expectations are based on pre-offer earnings, and when the accruals reverse subsequent to the offer, investors are disappointed with actual performance that results in a fall in the share price, lower than the initial earnings might have suggested. However, in studies of the banking industry, Wahlen (1994), Beaver and Engel (1996) and Liu and Ryan (1995) report that stock returns are negatively related to normal changes in loan loss provisions and positively related to abnormal loan loss provisions. From these studies, Healy and Wahlen (1999) infer that investors and shareholders suspect that firms with abnormally low loan loss provisions are managing earnings, and they discount the performance accordingly.

Dechow and Skinner (2000) identified a difference in attitude towards earnings management between regulators, practitioners and academics. Even before Enron and the other notorious scandals since 2001, regulators insisted that earnings management was a pervasive problem, and practitioners were confronted with it on a daily basis. However, empirical research did not support regulators' catastrophic implications of earnings management hypothesis. Consequently, the profession appeared to use this disagreement to justify inaction. In an attempt to reconcile the views of the three, Dechow and Skinner (2000) offered three reasons for the differing views. Their explanations focused largely on research design issues. First, because academics generally wish to make broad statements about earnings management, they choose large samples, and so tend to use statistical definitions of earnings management which may not be very powerful in identifying how it is effected. In contrast, practitioners observe earnings management almost daily. Second, the incentives tested by academics, such as loan covenants and bonus plans, are not of particular interest to practitioners and regulators and ex post are not very fruitful in identifying earnings management behaviour. Regulators in particular would rather focus on the 'meet or beat' incentive posed by the markets. Dechow and Skinner (2000) proposed that the final reason for the differing views stemmed from differing views on investor rationality. Academics frequently relied on the efficient markets hypothesis to argue that it 'did not matter' whether or not earnings management was disclosed, whereas regulators and practitioners had a more pragmatic view of investor knowledge and awareness.

McNichols (2000) contributed further insights to the research design issues in earnings management research. She suggested that the use of proxies was weak and that significant noise was introduced, which could vary over time and between industries, weakening the power of any research based on this approach. She also stated that studies that approached earnings management by examining the density of the distribution of earnings after they have been managed (eg. DeGeorge, 1999; Burgstahler and Eames, 1998; Burgstahler and Dichev, 1997) were silent on the incentives to manage earnings, and while they were more powerful than accruals proxy studies, they did not address where earnings were managed, why, or how frequently.

Despite the differing views, and the inconclusive empirical evidence on the impact of earnings management, there is no denying that recent evidence, and subsequent investigations, have revealed widespread earnings management. It appears that the scandals have borne out the pessimistic prediction of the Treadway Commission (1987, cited in Merchant and Rockness, 1994), that there was a danger over time that company financial reporting practices would sink to their lowest, most manipulative level. They have also vindicated the dire warnings advanced by the former SEC Chairman Arthur Levitt (Levitt, 1998; Loomis, 1999). Table 3.3 summarises a sample of the evidence from recent history.

Table 3.3 Financial scandals in which accounting firms were negatively cited (2002 – 2004)

Company	Auditor	Issue	Culpability/Action
Shell	KPMG & PwC	Overstated oil reserves, found to be incorrectly stated, had to be reduced by more than 20%.[3] The overstatement had inflated profits by $276 million.	External auditors (PwC and KPMG) are not required to sign off on oil reserves. However, despite this, reserves have a material effect on the bottom line and auditors are required to satisfy themselves that there are no major problems with the reserves. A newspaper report suggested that the affiliates to the international auditors were warned in 2002 about the possibility of problems.[4] Nonetheless, the group audit committee was advised that it could 'rely on the representations of the group's current management'.
ComRoad	KPMG	The company booked most of its sales between 1998 and 2000 to a non-existent company 'based' in Hong Kong.	KPMG did not issue a qualified audit report during that time. When the fraud was revealed (by management), KPMG resigned.

Table 3.3 Financial scandals in which accounting firms were negatively cited (2002 – 2004) (Continued)

Company	Auditor	Issue	Culpability/Action
Parmalat	Grant Thornton, Deloitte	Overstated earnings in 2002 and part of 2003, cash misstated by billions of dollars, company assets were 'negligible', and debt at US$2.3bn, was almost 8 times the amount directors reported. A subsequent investigation by prosecutors showed that Parmalat had only one profitable year between 1990 and 2001.[6]	A prosecutor's report indicated that Deloitte (who coordinated the worldwide audit) repeatedly ignored and buried evidence of accounting irregularities. They also failed to apply basic accounting principles and verify irregular and suspect entries. Two Grant Thornton employees were charged with fraud.
Xerox	KPMG	An SEC investigation concluded that Xerox was recognising revenue too early, thus allowing the company to achieve earnings targets it could not have otherwise met.[7]	A $10m no fault settlement was made with the SEC, however the SEC continued to sue KPMG and four partners, including the partner in charge of the audit on the grounds that they ignored warnings from colleagues and only 'meekly' challenged Xerox management.[8]

Table 3.3 Financial scandals in which accounting firms were negatively cited (2002 – 2004) (Continued)

Company	Auditor	Auditor	Culpability/Action
Gazprom	PwC	Mismanagement and asset-stripping, questioned by minority shareholders in Gazprom, but ignored save for an 'investigation' by the incumbent auditor PwC.[9]	Pricewaterhouse stands accused of producing false and misleading audits, by turning a blind eye to mismanagement and asset stripping at the company, including the sale of a gas field at below-market price and the lending of almost $1bn to outside companies, some of it interest free.
Élan	KPMG	Élan suffered a spectacular share price collapse after it was revealed that Élan was using joint ventures (located in havens such as Cayman and with almost no staff) to create 'round trip revenue' whilst keeping the related liability out of the accounts using complex technical consolidation rules in order to meet earnings targets.[10]	Both CEO and CFO at the time were former KPMG partners, and the auditor was, and remains, KPMG. Questions were raised as to whether KPMG's independence was compromised, and even whether the accounting was facilitated by the auditor but no action was taken against KMPG.

Table 3.3 Financial scandals in which accounting firms were negatively cited (2002 – 2004) (Continued)

Company	Auditor	Issue	Culpability/Action
Enron	Andersen	Special purpose entities were set up to hide billions of dollars of debt, severely overstating the company's share value, profits and reserves.	After the collapse of Enron Andersen was indicted on charges of obstruction of justice after it shredded 2 tonnes of documents relating to the Enron account at the prospect of an SEC investigation. It had audited and signed Enron's accounts without qualification since 1985. It was consulted and participated in the construction of the SPEs by the CFO. They violated both the substance of GAAP and the letter of GAAP.[11]
Qwest	Andersen	Company admitted improperly accounting for more than $1.1 billion of transactions from 1999 to 2001, which allowed it to show positive returns and maintain inflated stock price, generally by improperly engaging in capacity swaps with WorldCom and Enron, buying capacity it did not need.[12]	At a time when the price of fibre optics capacity was collapsing, this accounting technique was endorsed by Arthur Andersen, and it convinced investors that Qwest's growth prospects remained healthy.

Table 3.3 Financial scandals in which accounting firms were negatively cited (2002 – 2004) (Continued)

Company	Auditor	Issue	Culpability/Action
WorldCom	Andersen	WorldCom engaged in third party capacity swaps to maintain its growth image. Such swaps resulted in losses, which ought to have been recorded as expenses and were instead recorded as capital expenditure. This resulted in a misstatement of $4 billion[13 14].	The CFO made no attempt to cover up his frauds. Memos and emails candidly laid out the plans, however, congressional investigations revealed that Andersen was aware of this and took no action.
Global Crossing	Andersen	The SEC investigated how the energy giant recorded contract and capacity swaps in its books[15], and found that they were used to enhance revenue.	Andersen gave advice as to how to legitimise the transactions as fully as possible (applying market rates, etc) whilst being aware that the practice essentially drained the company of valuable assets.
Adelphia	Deloitte	Filed for bankruptcy protection and was being investigated by the SEC for related party transactions and self-dealing. Shortly before the collapse, it revealed inflated cash flow and revenue for 2000 and 2001 by more than $500 million.	It was argued that Deloitte were aware and failed to flag many of the related-party transactions, failed to consult with the audit committee on the complex cash systems, and had not provided the board with a management letter for 7 years.[16]

Table 3.3 Financial scandals in which accounting firms were negatively cited (2002 – 2004) (Continued)

Company	Auditor	Issue	Issue
Tyco	PwC	CEO was accused of fraud and insider trading.	Pricewaterhouse is understood to have known about many of the transactions, met with the accused parties, and determined that certain insider transactions did not need to be reported to the SEC.[17]
Peoplesoft	Ernst & Young	Between 1994 and 2001, E&Y was involved in a joint venture with Peoplesoft, for whom it also acted as auditor. An SEC investigation revealed that E&Y earned $425 million for implementing Peoplesoft software for third parties, that E&Y's tax group had an implementation partnership with Peoplesoft, and that in 1998 and 1999 alone, E&Y earned $150 million from implementing Peoplesoft software. In the same two years, E&Y earned $500,000 from auditing Peoplesoft, suggesting its capacity to act as an independent auditor was severely compromised.[18]	It was determined in the courts that E&Y partnered with Peoplesoft to the maximum extent possible to accomplish sales and boost consulting revenue. The SEC fined E&Y on the grounds that it had caused Peoplesoft to violate the requirement to engage an independent auditor, and also because E&Y's conduct was deemed to be negligent and reckless. E&Y was also barred from taking on new business for 6 months after the judgement.

The specific cases dealt with in this table have been discussed at length in both the professional and business press in recent years, in addition to being used as exemplars in much of the academic literature reviewed in this report. Consequently, they are not elaborated upon further in this section of the report.

Ethical dimensions of earnings management

> *The campaign to control creative accounting has put the spotlight on an issue that goes to the heart of business and legal ethics – the tendency to see minimalist compliance with advantageously interpreted regulation, literal compliance with the letter of the law, as good enough* (McBarnet and Whelan, 1999, p.275).

Earnings management is considered to be unethical, or at least unprofessional, by many (eg. Loomis, 1999; Levitt, 1998; Merchant and Rockness, 1994). Big 8/6/5 firms have been criticised for not standing up to clients with misleading financial statements (Dunn and Stewart, 1999; Schuetze, 1994; Briloff, 1990). While severely critical of auditor support of questionable accounting practices, Briloff (p.25) acknowledges that 'the accounting could be fully rationalised by GAAP - excepting that in each case ... form was given precedence over substance'. There is very little agreement on the ethicality of this type of earnings management (Kaplan, 2001). According to Staubus (2005, p.6), 'the dividing line between behavior that is acceptable and behavior that is unethical, or worse, is not always a bright one'.

The ethics of earnings management hinges on judgements of what is considered acceptable and what is not acceptable (Merchant and Rockness, 1994). In their empirical study of finance executives and internal auditors, acceptability was judged to vary with the type (operating vs accounting manipulations), size (materiality), timing (accounting period-end), and purpose (eg. to increase bonus) of the earnings management action. Previously, Merchant (1987) analysed some financial statement fraud cases to identify and chart a scale of acceptability of earnings management practices (acceptability continuum). At one extreme he identified practices, such as fraud, that virtually everyone would denounce as unacceptable. At the other end of the spectrum he included practices that most people would view as acceptable, such as, a fully disclosed change from accelerated to straight-line depreciation if 'the business is in need of more earnings'. Using interviews and panel-discussions with financial report preparers, users, auditors and regulators, Merchant (1987) listed six factors that affected people's placements of earnings management practices on the acceptability continuum.

- accordance with GAAP;
- clarity of intent to deceive;
- clarity of disclosure;
- materiality;
- period of effect; and
- direction.

Two studies focusing on the type of earnings management (Bruns and Merchant, 1990; Fischer and Rosenzweig, 1995) found a range of judgements about the acceptability of operating methods, as opposed to accounting methods, of managing earnings. Bruns and Merchant surveyed general, finance, and audit managers and Fischer and Rosenzweig used undergraduate accounting and MBA students, and accounting practitioners. Accounting manipulations were rated as more ethically unacceptable than operating manipulations. Students were more lenient in their judgements than those in practice, and it was speculated that this was due to the increased awareness afforded to practitioners by their experience at work.

To further test how Merchant's (1987) six factors affected people's placements of earnings management practices on the acceptability continuum, Merchant and Rockness (1994), used a questionnaire describing cases of potentially questionable earnings management activity, with senior financial employees of two major corporations and a sample of internal auditors. There were a number of key findings. First, there was widespread disagreement, both overall and within each group as to the general acceptability of earnings management, for example, in relation to deferring discretionary expenditure at year-end to achieve budget targets, just under 50% of respondents thought this action was acceptable, approximately one-third of respondents thought it unacceptable and the remainder were not sure. Second, ethical perceptions were affected by four of the six tested factors: type of action (operating or accounting); materiality; period of effect; and manager intent. Direction of effect (increase vs decrease earnings) and consistency with GAAP did not affect ethical perceptions. Third, employees from the corporation with a recent incidence of fraud were harsher in their judgement than the employees from the other corporation. Finally, general managers were most harsh in their judgements and internal auditors were most liberal. There was also some variety in the ranking of certain practices. Merchant and Rockness concluded that there was less than unanimous agreement about where the line between right and wrong should be drawn. Similar results were reported in Clikeman *et al.* (2001a) who used the same cases on a sample of students.

In an experimental study, extending Bruns and Merchant (1990) and Merchant and Rockness (1994), and testing the implications of Dye's (1988) model, Kaplan (2001) tested whether financial statement users' assessments of the ethicalness of earnings management was a function of intended benefit. He found that earnings management was assessed less unethically by shareholders for one of the three scenarios where the earnings management was intended for company benefit. In addition, intent did not influence ethicalness judgements among non-shareholders.

Consequently, he concluded that under certain conditions, shareholders and non-shareholders are influenced differently by the intent of earnings management.

Elias (2002) argues that there is a thin line separating earnings management and management fraud (see also Grant *et al.*, 2000; Levitt, 1998). Elias' study of CPAs, both in practice and in industry, and student CPAs assumed that earnings management typically fell somewhere between legitimacy and outright fraud. His results indicated that respondents believed that accounting manipulations of earnings were unethical, but that operating manipulations were not. Determinants of earnings management ethics, such as personal moral philosophies and social responsibility, were tested in this study. However, Elias concluded that while judgements on the ethicality of certain behaviour might be influenced by these determinants, the impact of these variables on behaviour or intention could not be predicted.

The effect of personal values on auditors' ethical decision-making was investigated in Shafer *et al.* (2001). They gave practising auditors scenarios involving client pressure on auditors to acquiesce in aggressive financial reporting. While expressing concern at the apparent willingness of respondents to permit manipulation of reported earnings, they concluded that personal value preferences did not influence ethical decision-making in auditing. However, they acknowledged limitations on the ability of personal values to explain or predict ethical judgements and behaviour. Nonetheless, their results provided support for the influence of moral intensity on auditors' decision processes and that auditors' ethical behaviour was 'strongly influenced by economic and utilitarian considerations' (p.273).

When considering the ethical ambiguity of earnings management, many academics refer to the 'slippery slope'. This phenomenon arises from individuals/firms failing to recognise the ethical issues or potential future ethical issues in a situation. An action is taken in the belief that it has little or no ethical consequences, but as the situation develops, over time, the issue becomes more serious than they first thought. They are then faced with two unpalatable choices: admit error or continue the action, even though they are less ethically comfortable with it (ICAS, 2004). It is this slippery slope that often carries minor ethical infractions into the territory of financial fraud. Indeed, this is echoed by the Treadway Commission (1987), which reported that most fraud begins with small ethical infractions. Karcher (1996) states that the single most effective way of avoiding the dangerous 'slippery slope' is to improve individuals' ethical sensitivity, and that this is the duty of firm managers, the profession, regulators, and educators. The first step towards this improvement is to assess the current prevailing morality regarding earnings management and the factors that contribute to that morality. To date, limited research has been conducted in this area.

Elias (2002) assesses the relationship between individuals' moral perceptions of earnings management and personal moral philosophies and the perceived role of ethics and social responsibility using accountants in practice and in industry, and students. As before, students were found to be more lenient than practitioners and all respondents rated accounting manipulations more harshly than operating manipulations. However, once more there was widespread disagreement as to the overall acceptability of earnings management. It was also found that perceptions of earnings management were positively correlated with idealism: high idealists rated earnings management more harshly and high relativists rated earnings management more leniently. It was also found that individuals who believed in corporate social responsibility and long-term gains rated earnings management more harshly, while those who believed in short-term gains rated such activities more leniently. This supports previous studies that have examined how other personal and environmental factors affect moral judgements of, and ethical sensitivity towards, earnings management, such as the tone at the top, locus of control, and organisational culture (ICAS, 2004; Roy, 1998).

Illegal activities

Apart from fraudulent financial reporting, the main areas of illegal activity with which accounting firms are associated in the literature are money laundering and tax evasion.

Lord Bingham, in the enquiry into the Bank of Credit and Commerce scandal in 1992, defined money laundering as transmitting 'illicit funds through the banking system in such a way as to disguise the origin or ownership of the funds' (cited in Mitchell *et al.*, 1998, p.590). Although relatively little research has addressed the 'antisocial and predatory acts of accountancy firms' (Mitchell *et al.*, 1998, p.590), researchers argue that the enormous amounts of money estimated to be laundered as a result of white collar crime, drug trafficking and tax evasion could not be successfully laundered without the involvement, expertise and advice of accountants, lawyers and financial advisors (Mitchell *et al.*, 1998; Willmott and Sikka, 1997).

Ethically questionable tax practices employed, promoted, or facilitated by large accountancy firms have existed for many decades, but their prevalence has increased as national and international wealth has increased. More recently, a four-volume report commissioned by the US Senate Finance Committee on the Enron collapse pointed to questionable practices by accounting, finance, and taxation advisors:

> *Big professional firms, investment banks and law firms - including Bankers Trust, Chase Manhattan, Deloitte & Touche and Andersen - gave Enron tax advice pushing legal boundaries* (Reynolds, 2003, p.57).

Reynolds argues that public perceptions of the ethics of the profession have been strained because of the scale of the wrongdoing and of the complexity of the devices used to fool others, which he claims 'almost beggar belief'. Accountancy firms have been implicated in tax frauds in many countries in recent years. For example, offshore accounts used to hide undeclared income, and bogus non-resident bank accounts used to avoid Deposit Income Retention Tax (DIRT) and to hide undeclared income were exposed in Ireland in the last decade and these have been investigated in long-running government established tribunals (Keena, 2002; Cahill, 2000). In both cases, large accountancy firms were cited for either participating as advisors to wealthy clients or for declining to expose this illegal activity.

Questionable tax activities, which are condoned and even promoted by accountancy firms, have also surfaced in the US. The boom of the late 1990s resulted in exceptional increases in individual and corporate wealth, which in turn boosted the demand for tax services, and in particular, strategies to minimise tax liabilities. During this period, the major accounting firms saw annual tax advisory revenue increase by 82% (Bryan-Low, 2004). Tax shelters devised by the tax arm of many accounting firms used complex derivatives, including warrants, options and swaps in questionable tax schemes. The tax authorities were not able to cope with this level of complexity. In particular, KPMG was accused of 'aggressively peddling their tax services', and being very aggressive in their strategies (Bryan-Low, 2004). One tax-partner noted in an internal memo that the use of certain tax strategies, combined with the reporting position advocated by KPMG, resulted in 'misleading, perhaps even false returns' (Bryan-Low, 2004). According to Bryan-Low, KPMG set up a telemarketing centre in the US to make cold calls to companies, to further sell their tax strategies. In one instance, a client faced with a capital gain of in excess of $28 million, used a tax shelter device developed by KPMG so that his tax returns filed showed a capital loss of more than $30 million. KPMG earned fees in excess of $600,000 for this one case. However, the authorities in the US clamped down on the use of these borderline strategies and KPMG was investigated by the Internal Revenue Service (IRS), the SEC and the Senate Permanent Committee on Investigations. The firm closed its telemarketing centre, ceased selling the aggressive shelters under investigation and admitted that:

> *...it helped wealthy individuals in the US to evade tax on billions of dollars of income and capital gains tax by selling them 'fraudulent' tax avoidance schemes'* (Irish Times, 2005).

KPMG was not alone in its attempt to abuse the US tax laws. PricewaterhouseCoopers settled with the IRS for an undisclosed sum, with no admission of wrong-doing, while Ernst & Young settled for $15 million, again with no admission of wrong-doing. Bryan-Low (2004) notes that the potentially abusive tax strategies, such as the ones marketed by KPMG, took billions from the US Treasury, and that one strategy in particular, cryptically labelled FLIP, reduced the federal tax take by $1.4 billion, and generated fees of at least $50 million.

Once more, there is limited empirical research investigating the relationship between taxation issues and accounting firm ethics. Jackson and Milliron (1986) conclude that there is a positive relationship between ethics and tax compliance. Hume *et al.* (1999) examine six ethical tax dilemmas and investigate whether CPA's use professional guidelines to resolve them, or whether they take the course of action which allows them to be loyal to the client. The results showed that a statistically significant number of CPAs did not follow the guidelines. However, the numbers were small, except in two cases: in the case of errors made by the current preparers on prior-year filings, 10% did not follow guidelines, and in the case of presenting estimates as rounded sums, 35% did not follow guidelines. Hume *et al.* suggest several reasons for the failure to follow guidelines, two of which are relevant in the context of ethics and the accounting firm. First, the CPAs did not perceive that their organisation, or the profession as a whole, considered the tax guidelines to be important. Secondly they might have failed to follow them because, as guidelines, there were few negative consequences or penalties for failing to adhere to them. When interpreting these findings, Beets and Killough (1990) note that CPAs failed to identify 25% of situations that conflicted with tax ethical guidelines, providing evidence that accountants do not always recognise an ethical issue when confronted with one.

Rules-based culture

> *A rules-based system reduces financial reporting to a mechanical exercise, within which devious people are sometimes tempted to cheat the spirit of the standards through the exploitation of loopholes. Standard-setters are then drawn into a downward spiral of avoidance and anti-avoidance, and before long, we all get bogged down in a quagmire of complexity and risk, losing sight of the overall view given by the accounts* (Paterson, 2004, p.35).

There are many references in the literature to the opinion that the hallmark of professionals is their ability to exercise good judgement (ICAS, 2006; McMillan, 2004). Nonetheless, accounting is perceived to be a rules-based profession (Pincus, 2000). Rules-based systems can be:

> *...a positive ethical force with many benefits, including consistency of decisions made by multiple decision-makers, promoting fairness, increasing predictability, and reducing uncertainty. However, ... rule-based systems are inherently sub-optimal* (Pincus, 2000, p.243).

Examples of sub-optimal behaviour, in either the absence of rules or in the presence of rules in accounting practice, are provided by Pincus. It is this paradox, whereby rules confer both benefits and dis-benefits, that convinces many commentators (eg. Duska, 2005; Staubus, 2004) that rationality and integrity must take precedence over rules to ensure good, ethical judgements prevail. It is argued in the literature that the many rules that have been created to 'guide' the work of the accountant have had the effect of 'deprofessionalising' the accountant because they remove the scope or need for exercising judgement and it has instead fostered a mechanical approach to auditing and financial reporting (ICAS, 2006; Staubus, 2004; West, 2003; Pincus, 2000; Briloff, 1986). Such an approach discourages, or even prevents auditors from looking beyond the standard set of questions, and in some situations allows the auditor to help clients to identify loopholes (Duska, 2005). Many auditors believe that their work is done once all the 'boxes' have been ticked, irrespective of whether other activities, not covered by the standard questions, are in keeping with the spirit of accounting and reporting standards and the fair view of financial reports. Being within the letter of the law appears to have become a sufficient criterion within accounting firms for competent delivery of responsibilities. Indeed, Duska (2005) argues that wealth accumulation and a dismissal of traditional auditor responsibilities, had led to a compliance culture without a sense of ethical responsibility.

In the context of discussing whether or not accounting is a profession, Staubus (2004) discusses West's (2003) contention that the accounting profession's control over the rule-making process is, if not oblivious of the public interest, then at least independent of a sharp focus on it. According to Staubus (2004, p.146), West argues that 'the accounting profession looks at the making and application of rules as performing its duty'.

Whilst not suggesting that accountants were more moral at the turn of the 20th century, Preston *et al.* (1995) analysed and contrasted the processes and discussions surrounding the development of the AICPA's ethical codes in 1917 and 1988 and concluded as follows:

> *...the code, the discourses surrounding it, and thus the very conceptualisation of what constitutes morality within the accounting profession have undergone a number of profound changes. The overtly moral discourse at the turn of the century, in which we observe reflections upon the ten commandments, right and wrong,*

> *the virtues of courage, loyalty, integrity, duty, responsibility and the professional state of mind, stands in somewhat stark contrast to current concerns over what rules members ought to follow, what standards ought to be set and adhered to, and what solid media hits, advertising campaigns and public relations tools ought to be deployed to shape public perceptions* (Preston *et al.*, 1995, p.536).

Abbott (1988) identified that a distinguishing characteristic of a professional was the ability to exercise the art of inference between the diagnosis of a situation and the decision on the treatment required in a particular instance. McMillan (2004, p.948) adapts this to accountancy when he states 'the professionalism of an accountant refers to the ability to make prudent and just inferences'. Accepting that judgement is generally required when expressing an opinion on the fairness of accounts, McMillan (2004) argues nonetheless, that seven decades of rule-making in accounting and auditing 'have created the probability of future failures'. This may well be because:

> *...practising accountants sometimes have a genuine conflict between duties to refrain from rules violations and duties to disclose information in the public interest* (Ruland and Lindblom, 1992, p.268).

In an analysis of accountants' duties and responsibilities using criteria identified from philosophy, Ruland and Lindblom (1992) concluded that the four criteria of relentlessness (the duty to disclose all relevant information is relentless and can never be fully satisfied), certainty, responsibility, and magnitude combine to create a disclosure imperative in some circumstances and not in others. All except the first criterion serve to define and limit the circumstances under which there is a duty to disclose. Using the savings and loan scandal in the US as an example,

Ruland and Lindblom conclude that compliance with GAAP did not absolve accountants of their ethical duty to disclose information which was important for the public interest. Accountants can be obliged to violate rules of professional conduct requiring client confidentiality or compliance with GAAP in order to disclose information which is in the public interest.

Nelson *et al.* (2002) concluded that managers were more likely to attempt earnings management and auditors were less likely to adjust for these attempts when the earnings management was either structured, such as by modifying contracts, transactions, or activities, with respect to precise standards, or unstructured with respect to imprecise standards. Audit engagement partners have been shown to rely on rules to support their position when serious issues arise between the auditor and the finance director. In a study which investigated how auditors and finance directors resolved serious differences, Beattie et al. (2004, p.16) stated that:

> *...[a] well researched argument grounded in the regulations greatly helped the AEP [audit engagement partner] to carry his point. Where the issue was a matter of judgement rather than a straightforward matter of compliance with a regulation, the AEP found it more difficult to get his point of view accepted.*

Despite ever increasing regulation in response to various capital market crises, it is often argued that it is counter-productive to continually add layer upon layer to the rule-book (Williams, 2004; Pincus, 2000). Williams (2004, p.996) argues that the modern emphasis on technical accounting rules has been morally detrimental in addition to being potentially futile, as follows:

> *A serious consequence of this modern accounting discourse has been the transformation in the academy of the accounting function from*

> *an essentially moral or legal one to a purely technical one, which has no robust technical foundations.*

Similarly, Paterson (2004) argues for a greater emphasis on ethical values:

> *What we need is not more rules – we are positively drowning in them – but a renewed emphasis on the ethical values on which our profession is founded. … if Enron demonstrates one thing, it is that prescriptive regulation is no guarantor of reliable accounting, and it might even conspire to undermine it.*

McMillan (2004, p.949) supports these views and refers to the limitation of responding to audit and accountancy failures by imposing more enclosure type controls, which specify within the rules what is allowed and what is prohibited, because:

> *…it [imposing more enclosure type controls] eliminates the need to develop within the individual auditor and the accounting firm an even keener moral calculus of the appropriateness of the auditor's actions with the client in relationship to its greater social role: to attest to the veracity of management's financial statements.*

Accounting education is also criticised for its focus on accounting rules. A succinct expression of this criticism is provided by Revsine (2002, p.143), as follows:

> *Accounting education's greatest failure is in training auditors. ….. in order to perform competent audits, auditors must be 'financial detectives'. But how can they become financial detectives when they are clueless regarding the economic environment, managerial incentives, strategic gaming and other business realities that were*

omitted from the rules-driven upper level courses many were exposed to.

However, Amernic and Craig (2004, p.348) caution on the possible disconnect between understanding principles of ethical and moral behaviour and actual behaviour in business and professional contexts where commercial and cultural pressures and domination by professional rules can pervert well-meaning auditors.

> *It is folly to argue that the failures of Enron, WorldCom and their like occurred because of a few rogue accountants and corporate executives who didn't receive sufficient dollops of 'ethics' as undergraduates or MBAs; and/or because US GAAP was too 'rule-bound'. ....Even if auditors were educated to be ethical and moral .... and, in their professional lives as auditors, were 'as honest as possible, [had] impeccable integrity and [were] competent and intrepid to the hilt', the fact that they follow and endorse generally accepted accounting rules and practices means that 'almost certainly they will be signing off on what mostly is financial nonsense!'* (Dean *et al.*, 2002, p.iii).

Summary

Given the difficulty of specifying the meaning of ethics in the context of the professional firm, the literature reviewed in this chapter has concentrated on issues and aspects of accounting firm activities most heavily criticised in the literature in the wake of the financial and accounting scandals of recent years. This includes the commercial ethos of accounting firms, which has been blamed for firms losing sight of their responsibilities as professionals with a commitment to acting in the public interest, the perceived conflicts of interest arising from the multiplicity of services provided by accountancy firms and the accusation that accounting firms compromise the required standards of integrity and objectivity, and sometimes the quality of the work performed.

In addition to exploring the commercial pressures on the traditional notion of professional behaviour and the consequences of the ever-increasing emphasis on commercial success of accounting practices in this chapter, the literature review includes an overview of auditor independence and audit quality, earnings management, lobbying and the association of accounting firms with illegal activities. This wide range of literature demonstrates unethical behaviour by accounting firms. In many cases, the areas around which substantial criticism of accounting firms is commonplace have been researched from an economic consequences perspective rather than from an ethical or moral framing point of view. In addition, many of the concepts, such as independence and quality, cannot be measured or directly identified. To the extent that they have been investigated empirically, proxies have been used with limited efficacy.

Because of their privileged access to providing external audit services and the dependence of external stakeholders on the integrity of the opinions provided through that process, it is frequently argued in the literature that accounting firms can, and do, fail in their ethical responsibilities to those who technically appoint them and to other stakeholders who rely on them to underwrite the efficiency and effectiveness of the capitalist system. The many financial and accounting scandals of the recent past, coupled with the extinction of the major accounting firm Arthur Andersen, provide ample evidence of flaws in the standard of service provided by accounting firms. Whether these flaws are described as ethical failures, quality control failures, or management control failures by accounting firms is somewhat academic. The consensus in the literature is that these events demonstrate that a redoubling of effort to operate professionally is essential to restore public confidence in the accounting profession in general, and accounting firms in particular.

References to the 'deprofessionalisation' of accounting abound in the literature. It is suggested that the existence of excessive rules limits the extent to which the exercise of judgement is permitted or required. However, it is also suggested that contemporary accountants are either unable or unwilling to exercise judgement, for example, in relation to whether or not earnings management is compatible with the 'true and fair' view required of financial statements in Europe, or whether or not independence is impaired by close ties with management of audit clients. Accountants appear to disagree on the acceptability of earnings management, client advocacy and lobbying, and the provision of advice on tax shelters. There is some evidence that they fail to recognise the ethical consequences of such practices.

Endnotes

1. This accusation is explicitly stated in McMillan (2004, p.944) when he followed a brief discussion of the complexity of the financial reporting system (and its abuse by participants in Enron, Qwest, Global Crossing and others) with: 'The profession was participating directly in providing their valuable clients with means to deceive the public.' Reinstein and McMillan (2004, p.957) were also explicit when they stated that '... public accountants have often helped their clients paint too rosy a picture by misapplying vague, arbitrary accounting rules.'

2. Specifically, threats to western capitalist industry caused by the oil crisis of 1970s, and competitive pressures from more efficient and lower cost economies such as Japan in 1980s have been characterised as economic 'shocks'. Attempts by business and governments to respond to these 'shocks' included privatization, rationalization, introduction of 'managerialism' into public sector organizations such as hospitals, universities, and into other organizations such as charities.

3. Herrick, T and M Schroeder (2004), 'Shell cuts estimate of reserves again, delays SEC filing', Wall Street Journal Europe, 12-14 March.

4. Cummins, C (2004), 'Shell outside auditors got reserves warning in 2002', Wall Street Journal Europe, 15 July.

5. Lynn, M (2004), 'One accounting scandal in less than a year might be an accident. Two could be a coincidence. But three starts to look as if something is wrong with the system' The Sunday Times, 18 January.

6. Roberts, R Y, R P Swanson and J Dinneen (2004), 'Spilt milk: Parmalat and Sarbanes-Oxley internal controls reporting', International Journal of Disclosure and Governance, Vol.1(3), pp.215-233.

7. Anonymous, (2003), 'Flawed action but ghosts remain', Accounting & Business, March.

8. Anonymous, (2003), 'SEC targets KPMG methods', The Irish Times, 30 January.

9. Whalen, J and G Chazen (2002), 'Gazprom shareholder files suits against Pricewaterhouse', Wall Street Journal Europe, 16 April.

10. Pierce, A (2003), 'Élan Corporation: A case study in corporate obfuscation', Corporate Governance International, Vol.6(1), pp.5-23.

11. Benston, G J and A L Hargreaves (2002), 'Enron: What happened and what we can learn from it', Journal of Accounting and Public Policy, Vol.21, pp.105-127.

12. O'Clery, C (2002), 'Qwest executives made fortunes in stock sales as firm floundered', The Irish Times, 31 July.

13. Anonymous, (2002), 'Andersen plays WorldCom victim card', The Irish Times, 27 June.

14. Moloney, E (2002), 'This one could run and run', The Sunday Tribune, 30 June.

15. Berman, D K and D Soloman (2002), 'Accounting questions surround the telecom pioneer', Wall Street Journal Europe, 14 February.

16. Soloman, D (2002), 'Adelphia board seeks to drop Deloitte as company's auditor', Wall Street Journal Europe, 10 June.

17. Mumma, C (2003), 'PwC is accused of inaction in Tyco case', The Sunday Tribune, 9 February.

18. Friedland, J (2004), 'Comment: Time to end the Big Four cartel', International Journal of Disclosure and Governance, Vol.1(3), pp.211- 213.

Chapter Four

Conclusions

This literature review has identified the issues that have been raised, researched and critiqued in the academic, professional and business literatures in relation to 'ethics and the professional accounting firm'. The topic itself is very broad and covers a range of relevant literatures and research paradigms. However, there is a paucity of research focusing directly on accounting firms in general, and the ethics of their practices and influences, in particular.

This review involved identifying the standard of behaviour that might be legitimately expected of accounting firms in the context of the historical background, professional status, legal and State recognition given to auditors, and self-proclamations by practitioners and their representatives. Using these expectations as a benchmark, specific aspects of accounting firms' *modus operandi* were explored through the literature with a view to evaluating whether accounting firms lived up to, or fell short of, these expectations. Aspects examined included the modern commercial focus of accounting firms, their broad service provision orientation, their willingness to act as advocates for client management and their sometimes ambivalent attitudes towards earnings management, questionable tax shelters and issues of auditor independence.

The characteristics, behaviours and ethos surrounding accounting firms were outlined in chapters one and two. Traits such as objectivity, independence, integrity and occupational expertise are identified in the literature as typical of the ideal accounting practitioner, as well as prioritising the public interest over self-interest. These behavioural characteristics are valued by accountants and accountancy firms. Although they are not exclusively found among professionally qualified groups of people, they are identified in the literature as the hallmarks of professional accountants to which accounting firms refer when pursuing recognition for themselves and as a defense against threats and criticism, and staking claims to superiority in a variety of contexts. A code of professional ethics has traditionally underpinned such claims, although the literature provides evidence of cynical manipulation of such codes and associated rules to facilitate the broadening scope of accounting firms' work. Such manipulation of ethical codes has been characterised in the literature as prioritising the self-interest of accounting practitioners over the public interest, and of legitimising activities not previously considered within the scope of ethical practice. The broadening scope of accounting firms' work has not only been criticised because of its threat to auditor independence, but also for the authority it gives the accountancy profession, and the business culture that their advice often reflects, over societal policies and priorities.

The literature suggests that there are ongoing conflicts between what the profession and accountancy firms think will advance their cause and what the profession is prepared to do to ensure that members and member firms live up to the ideal professional model. A commitment from the profession to calling unethical activities and behaviour by accounting firms unethical, and to imposing penalties that will act as deterrents is essential to promote shared ethical values. It is widely argued in the literature that these values are of long-term and fundamental importance to the reputation of accounting firms. There is also evidence of ongoing conflict between the practical reality – or commercial imperative - of many professional firms, particularly the larger ones, adopting the business/managerial model rather than the more traditional, and possibly naïve concept of a professional practice that provides expert service in the public interest. Furthermore, the literature suggests that, given the expansion in numbers joining the profession, particularly since the late-1960s, it may be unreasonable to expect that something as subtle as a sense of professionalism will drive appropriate behaviour.

In order to establish the extent to which accounting firms have lived up to, or fallen short of, legitimate expectations of ethical behaviour, the critical, sociological and business ethics literatures were reviewed in chapter three, in addition to some empirical research addressing auditor independence issues and aspects of earnings management. The overarching theme of this chapter is the extent to which the responses of accounting firms to available commercial opportunities in the last third of the 20th century exerted pressure on the traditional core values of accounting firms. Evidence on the impairment of independence and objectivity by providing non-audit services to audit clients is mixed. However, there is clearly substantial concern that auditor independence is not adequately protected or prioritised by accounting firms in the face of commercial opportunities. Consequently, the reliability of the external audit opinion on financial statements is exposed to doubts. This has serious consequences for governance systems underlying capitalist economies.

Analyses of the current problems in financial reporting and auditing are plentiful in the recent literature (see eg. Rezaee, 2005; Friedland, 2004; Copeland, 2003; Benston and Hartgraves, 2002; Sutton, 2002). Evidence of an integrity deficit is generally anecdotal or based on reasoned argument surrounding commentary and investigations of the financial scandals of recent years. Evidence of conflicts of interest is provided in the literature, as is evidence of perceptions that independence has been impaired by many of the activities and *modus operandi* of accounting firms in recent decades. In addition, the association of accounting firms with illegal activities such as money-laundering and illegal tax shelters is undeniably evidence of unethical behaviour.

Among the proposals for reform affecting audit firms are suggestions:

- investors hire and fire external auditors directly (see Mayhew and Pike, 2004; Staubus, 2004);

- auditors concentrate on the core audit and assurance services and abandon their commercial focus (Hermanson and Lapides, 2003);
- the tone at the top of audit firms changes; and
- greater effort should be given to ensuring that 'clients meet the intent of the applicable accounting standards', and less effort to assisting clients to 'structure transactions to avoid the intent of standards' (Wyatt, 2004, p.51).

The importance of skepticism and questioning to effective auditing has been reiterated in the context of criticisms that audit firms incorrectly focus on pleasing client firm management and are too beholding to them because of management's control over hiring and firing auditors and over consulting appointments.

According to Abbott (1988), the essence of a profession is to exercise the art of inference between the diagnosis of a situation and the decision on the treatment required in the particular instance. In other words, the hallmark of professionals is their ability to exercise good judgement (McMillan, 2004; ICAS, 2006). It is argued in the literature that the many rules which have been created to guide the work of the accountant have had the effect of 'de-professionalising' the accountant because they remove the scope or need for exercising judgement. They have, instead, fostered a mechanical approach to auditing and financial reporting. Such an approach discourages or even prevents auditors from looking beyond the standard set of questions, and in some situations, allows the auditor to help clients identify loopholes, and allows them to believe that their work is done once all the 'boxes' have been ticked, irrespective of whether other activities, not covered by the standard questions, are in-keeping with the spirit of accounting and auditing standards and the fair view of financial performance and position. For many accounting firms, the literature suggests that being within the letter of the law appears to have become sufficient for the competent delivery of responsibilities. It is argued that the traditional focus on accounting as a primarily technical discipline desensitises entrants to the profession to the moral aspects of their work, thus making it difficult for accountants to make moral judgements (Mayper *et al.*, 2005).

The loss of respect for US accounting practitioners over time is described by Zeff (2003b) as a 'descent under stress'. He identifies the following as contributory factors:

- scandals causing losses to investors and questioning of auditors' role;
- court cases contributing to loss of auditor backbone;
- loss of standard-setting role in US on formation of FASB and consequent withdrawal of leading professionals from discourse surrounding accounting principles;
- congressional criticism;
- pressure to alter competitive climate; and
- burgeoning consulting services.

The critical and sociological literature reviewed in this report expresses a somewhat depressing prognosis for the future of the accountancy profession given the evidence of marginalisation at best, and irrelevance at worst, of traditional professional characteristics and values in the *modus operandi* of contemporary accounting firms. An example of this bleak outlook comes from Boyd (2004, p.393):

> *All of the evidence suggests that the modern evolution of the accountancy profession has been down a one-way street, and that a voluntary reversal of this evolution back towards an era of greater professional integrity would be extremely hard to effect. The future evolution of the profession would appear to be in the hands of external regulators and legislators, implying that the*

fundament of any profession, self-regulation, is forever lost to the accounting profession.

The cumulative effect on the accountancy profession of systemic reforms throughout the 20th century and most especially in the early years of the 21st century, has been the gradual loss of the right to self-regulate. The far-reaching effects of Sarbanes-Oxley legislation mean that this legislation has been felt by accounting firms and listed companies world-wide. Ironically, although the legislation imposes extensive inspection, monitoring and accountability on accounting firms, there is anecdotal evidence that it has also increased their profitability, at least in the short-term.

In the context of ethics and the professional firm, the literature provides substantial criticism of conflicts of interest within the public practice of accounting. To the extent that conflicts of interest impair auditor independence, they represent ethical dilemmas. Given the difficulty of identifying, testing and proving independence, limited concrete evidence that accounting firms have behaved unethically is available in the literature. However, evidence is provided that accounting firms are perceived to be unethical in many of their contemporary business practices.

The literature on professions and professionalism, and on professional ethics suggest that honesty, objectivity and fairness are essential characteristics for ethical practice in accounting. Substantive questions arise in the literature concerning the honesty, objectivity and fairness of accounting firms in the context of earnings management and the provision of non-audit services to audit clients. The ethicality of earnings management is a complex question, which has only begun to be addressed in the academic research. Results of the research addressing this question to date, are mixed. More research adopting a greater variety of research methods and an extension of the prior research approaches to more comprehensively accommodate the complexities of 'earnings management' and 'ethicality' is necessary to investigate the range of practices and tolerances falling under this heading.

The research examined for this report identified the very successful commercialisation of accountancy and related services as the main driver of the change of ethos within accounting firms from a predominantly 'service in the public interest' mindset to a 'commercial business, profit maximising' culture. Some argue that over time the statutory audit function has been relegated in importance to accounting firms because of its relatively low contribution to profitability. Nonetheless, its importance as an entry to more lucrative business and as a signal of the valuable skills provided by accounting firms is acknowledged in the literature. The tensions created by the firms' pursuit of profit and growth targets undermine traditional values to the point where differentiation by professional status is seriously questioned in the literature.

Given the complexity of the relevant social constructs investigated in the literature in this report, such as ethics, independence and quality, direct measurement is generally impossible and cause-effect relationships are confounded by the myriad of environmental influences that surround them. While both scientific and qualitative research approaches are adopted in the research reviewed, each has strengths and weaknesses in the context of the questions being pursued, potential access to relevant data, and validity of conclusions drawn. Some of the more scientific research reported adopts more or less plausible proxies for concepts such as independence, audit quality and earnings management, that cannot be directly measured or where access to facts is impossible. Consequently, conclusions from research using relatively sophisticated research methods must be interpreted in the context of the weakness of the proxies used.

Investigation of behaviour impacting on ethics and accounting firms typically depends on archival, questionnaire, interview, and experimental methodologies. This qualitative research often includes perceptions gathered by interviews and the completion of questionnaires.

Alternatively, inferences are drawn from the analysis of archival data or laboratory experiments. Limitations of this type of research include social response bias, non-response bias, and the artificiality of scenarios and experiments. Consequently, the benefit of potentially richer real-life in-depth investigations grounded in context, is somewhat counter-balanced by these methodological limitations.

The research reviewed in this report raises more questions than it answers. This suggests that a substantial and varied research agenda can, and possibly ought, to be pursued surrounding the topic of 'ethics and the accounting firm'. Among the questions for which either incomplete answers or no answers are provided by the extant literature, are the following:

- Is there any difference between a profession and an industry in the 21st century?
- Should expectations of public practice of accounting be different from those of other specialist service providers?
- Can the focus on commercial success by professional firms be reconciled with high moral standards?
- Can independence in fact be identified, quantified and measured?
- Should audit firms be more accountable to shareholders/other stakeholders than they are at present?
- Can moral character be institutionalised in an accounting firm?
- Is zero-tolerance for unethical behaviour in accounting firms reasonable?
- Can the ethicality of earnings management be determined?

Greater research access to accounting firm personnel at all levels, and to firm policies and practices will be required to rigorously investigate some of the research issues prompted by this review. In particular, the following research questions need to be addressed to help frame and inform accounting firm and professional body strategic policies geared towards superior professional performance:

- How does an accounting firm culture develop and spread?
- What determines 'good' accounting firm culture and 'bad' accounting firm culture?
- Are robust moral targets achievable and sustainable in accounting firms in a world where value sets change frequently?

Reputation and integrity are at the heart of the value added by auditors to financial and other reports. Actual or perceived unethical behaviour diminishes the collective reputations of accountants, accounting firms and the accounting profession. O'Connell (2004, p.746) offered a quotation from Socrates as a reminder of the relationship between reputation and professional credibility. It provides food for thought at the conclusion of this report:

> *Regard your good name as the richest jewel you can possibly be possessed of – for credit is like fire; when once you have kindled it you may easily preserve it, but if you once extinguish it, you will find it an arduous task to rekindle it again. The way to gain a good reputation is to endeavour to be what you desire to appear.*

References

Abernethy, M A and J U Stoelwinder (1995), 'The role of professional control in the management of complex organizations', *Accounting, Organizations and Society*, Vol.20(1), pp.1-17.

Abbott, A (1988), 'The System of Professions: An essay on the division of Expert Labor', *University of Chicago Press*, Chicago.

Abbott, A (1983), 'Professional Ethics', *American Journal of Sociology*, Vol.88(5), pp.855-885.

Abbott, L J, S Parker, G F Peters and D V Rama (2003), 'Audit, Nonaudit, and Information Technology fees: some empirical evidence', *Accounting and Public Interest*, Vol.3, pp.1-20.

Abdel-khalik, A R (2002), 'Reforming corporate governance post Enron: Shareholders' Board of Trustees and the auditor', *Journal of Accounting and Public Policy*, Vol.21(2), pp.97-103.

Abdolmohammadi, M J, W J Read and D P Scarbrough (2003), 'Does selection-socialization help to explain accountants' weak ethical reasoning?', *Journal of Business Ethics*, Vol.42(1), pp.71 - 81.

Ahadiat, N and J J Mackie (1993), 'Ethics Education in Accounting: An investigation of the importance of ethics as a factor in the recruiting decisions of public accounting firms', *Journal of Accounting Education*, Vol.11(2), pp.243-257.

AICPA (1988), *Education requirements for entry into the accounting profession*, 2nd edition, AICPA, New York.

Alderman, C W and J W Deitrick (1982), 'Auditors' Perceptions of Time Budget Pressures and Premature Sign-offs: A Replication and Extension', *Auditing: A Journal of Practice & Theory*, Vol.1(Fall), pp.54-68.

Alexander, J A and T D'Aunno (1990), 'Transformation of institutional environments: Perspectives on the corporatization of U.S health care' in Mick, S (ed), *Innovations in Health Care Delivery*, pp.53-85, Jossey-Bass, San Francisco, CA.

Allen, K (1991), 'In Pursuit of Professional Dominance: Australian Accounting 1953 –1985', *Accounting Auditing & Accountability Journal*, Vol.4(1), pp.51-67.

Amernic, J and R Craig (2004), 'Reform of Accounting Education in the Post-Enron Era: Moving Accounting 'Out of the Shadows'', *Abacus*, Vol.40(3), pp.342 – 378.

Anderson, U, K Kadous and L Koonce (2004), 'The role of incentives to manage earnings and quantification in auditors' evaluations of management-provided information', *Auditing: A Journal of Practice & Theory*, Vol.23(1), pp.11-27.

Anderson-Gough, F, C Grey and K Robson (2001), 'Tests of time: organizational time-reckoning and the making of accountants in two multi-national accounting firms', *Accounting, Organizations and Society*, Vol.26(2), pp.99-122.

Andrew, R (1988), 'High Stakes', *CA Magazine*, September, pp.23-28.

Antle, R (1999), 'Accounting firms, the accounting industry, and accounting research', *British Accounting Review*, Vol.31(1), pp.1-13.

APB (Auditing Practices Board) (2004), *Ethical Standards for Auditors (ES1-5)*, APB, London.

Armstrong M B (1987) 'Moral Development and Accounting Education', *Journal of Accounting Education*, Vol.5(1), pp.27-43.

Armstrong, P (1985), 'Changing Management control strategies: The role of competition between accountancy and other organisational professions', *Accounting, Organizations and Society*, Vol.10(2), pp.129-148.

Arnold, P and P Sikka (2001), 'Globalization and the state-profession relationship: The case of the Bank of Credit and Commerce International', *Accounting, Organizations and Society*, Vol.26(6), pp.475-99.

Arnold D F Sr., R A Bernardi and P E Neidermeyer (1999), 'The effect of independence on decisions concerning additional audit work: A European Perspective', *Auditing: A Journal of Practice & Theory*, Vol.18(supplement), pp.45-67.

Ashbaugh, H, R LaFond and B W Mayhew (2003), 'Do Nonaudit Services compromise Auditor Independence? Further Evidence', *The Accounting Review*, Vol.78(3), pp.611-639.

Axline L L (1990), 'The bottom line on ethics: A fresh perspective on a worthwhile subject', *Journal of Accountancy*, December, pp.87-91.

Baggott, R (1989), 'Regulatory reform in Britain: The changing face of self-regulation', *Public Administration*, Winter, Vol.67, pp.435-454.

Baker, R C (2005), 'What do we mean by accounting for the public interest?', *In the Public Interest*, Vol.33(2), pp1-2.

Baker, R C (2004), '*What do we mean by accounting for the public interest?*', Paper presented at the Fourth Asia Pacific Interdisciplinary Research in Accounting Conference, Singapore.

Baker R C (2001), 'Whether there is an accounting profession? A commentary on 'Whither (or wither) accounting education in the new millennium' by M.R. Mathews', *Accounting Forum*, Vol.25(4), pp.402-404.

Baker R C (1993), 'Self-regulation in the public accounting profession: The structural response of the large public accounting firms to a changing environment', Accounting, Auditing & Accountability Journal, Vol.6(2), pp.68-80.

Baker R C (1977), 'Management strategy in a large accountancy firm', The Accounting Review, July, pp.576–586.

Baker, T, D Collins and A Reitenga (2003), 'Stock option compensation and earnings management incentives', *Journal of Accounting, Auditing & Finance*, Vol.18(4), pp.557-582.

Bartels, R (1967), 'A Model for Ethics in Marketing', *Journal of Marketing*, Vol.31, pp.20-26.

Bazerman, M H, G Loewenstein and D A Moore (2002), 'Why good accountants do bad audits', *Harvard Business Review*, November, Vol.11(1), pp.72–98.

Beasley M S, J V Carcello and D R Hermanson (1999), *Fraudulent Financial Reporting 1987 – 1997: An Analysis of U.S. Public Companies*, COSO.

Beattie, V, R Brandt and S Fearnley (1999), 'Perceptions of auditor independence', *Journal of International Accounting, Auditing & Taxation*, Vol.8(1), pp.67–107.

Beattie, V, R Brandt and S Fearnley (1998), 'Auditor independence and the expectations gap: Some evidence of changing user perceptions', *Journal of Financial Regulation and Compliance*, Vol.6(2), pp.159 – 170.

Beattie, V, A Goodacre and S Fearnley (2003), 'And then there were four: A study of UK audit market concentration – causes, consequences and the scope for market adjustment', *Journal of Financial Regulation and Compliance*, Vol.11(3), pp.250-265.

Beattie, V and S Fearnley (2002), *Auditor Independence and Non-Audit Services: A Literature Review*, ICAEW, London, available at: http://www.icaew.co.uk/viewer/index.cfm?AUB=TB2I_63270.

Beattie, V, S Fearnley and R Brandt (2004), 'A grounded theory model of auditor-client negotiations', *International Journal of Auditing*, Vol.8, pp.1-19.

Beattie, V, S Fearnley and R Brandt (2001), *Behind closed doors: What company audit is really about*, Palgrave and ICAEW, London, pp. xxii + 309.

Beattie, V, S Fearnley and R Brandt (2000), 'Behind the audit report: A descriptive study of discussions and negotiations between auditors and directors', *International Journal of Auditing*, Vol. 4, pp.177-202.

Beaver, W. and E. Engel, (1996), 'Discretionary behaviour with respect to allowances for loan losses and the behaviour of security prices', *Journal of Accounting and Economics*, Vol. 22, pp.177-206.

Bédard, J (2001), 'The disciplinary process of the accounting profession: protecting the public or the profession? The Quebec experience', *Journal of Accounting and Public Policy*, Winter, Vol.20(4-5), pp.399-437.

Bédard, J and Y Gendron (2004), 'Qualitative Research on Accounting: Some Thoughts on What Occurs Behind the Scene', in Humphrey, C and B. Lee (eds), *The Real Life Guide to Accounting Research: A Behind-the-Scenes View of using Qualitative Research Methods*, Elsevier, Amsterdam.

Beets S D and L N Killough (1990), 'The effectiveness of a compliant-based ethics enforcement system: Evidence from the accounting profession', *Journal of Business Ethics*, Vol. 9(2), pp.115-126.

Benston, G J and A L Hartgraves (2002), 'Enron: what happened and what we can learn from it', *Journal of Accounting and Public Policy*, Vol.21(2), pp.105-127.

Bews, N F and G J Rossouw (2002), 'A role for business ethics in facilitating trustworthiness', *Journal of Business Ethics,* Vol.39(4), pp.377-390.

Boyd, C (2004), 'The structural origins of conflicts of interest in the accounting profession', *Business Ethics Quarterly*, Vol.14(3), pp.377-398.

Briloff, A J (2004), 'Accounting scholars in the groves of academe: In Pari Delicto', *Critical Perspectives on Accounting*, Vol.15(6/7), pp.787-796.

Briloff, A J (2001), 'Garbage in/Garbage out: A critique of fraudulent financial reporting: 1987 - 1997 (the COSO report) and the SEC accounting regulatory process', *Critical Perspectives on Accounting*, Vol.12(2), pp125-148.

Briloff, A J (1990), 'Accountancy and Society: A Covenant Desecrated', *Critical Perspectives on Accounting*, Vol.1(1), pp.5-30.

Briloff, A J (1986), 'Accountancy and the public interest', *Advances in Public Interest Accounting*, Vol.1, pp.1-14.

Briloff, A J (1972) *Unaccountable Accounting: Games Accountants Play*, Harper & Row, New York.

Brinkmann, J and K Ims (2003), 'Good intentions aside: drafting a functionalist look at codes of ethics', *Business Ethics: A European Review*, Vol.12(3), pp.265-274.

Brinkmann, J (2002), 'Marketing ethics as professional ethics: Concepts, approaches and typologies', *Journal of Business Ethics*, Vol.41(1/2), pp.159-177.

Bromell, T (2004), 'Taking an ethical lead', *Accountancy*, September, pp.130-131.

Brown, K (2002), 'Audit Methods Make it Hard to Uncover Fraud', *The Wall Street Journal Europe*, 9 July.

Brown, K and I J Dugan (2002), 'Sad Account: Anderson's Fall from Grace', *The Wall Street Journal Europe*, 10 June.

Brown, L D (1998), *Managerial behaviour and the bias in analyst forecasts*, Working Paper, Georgia State University.

Brown, R E (2005) 'Enron/Andersen: Crisis in U.S. Accounting and Lessons for Government', *Public Budgeting and Finance*, Fall, pp.20-32.

Bruce, R (1996), 'Whiter than White', *Accountancy International*, May, pp56-57.

Bruns, W J and K A Merchant (1990), 'The dangerous morality of managing earnings', *Management Accounting*, August, pp.22-25.

Bryan-Low, C (2004), 'KPMG, Other U.S. Audit Firms Face Fallout From Tax Shelters', *The Wall Street Journal Europe*, 12-14 July.

Bryan-Low, C (2002), 'Study finds Auditing Firms Fail to Unfurl Red Flags', *The Wall Street Journal Europe*, 26 February.

Burgstahler, D (1997), *Incentives to manage earnings to avoid earnings decreases and losses: Evidence from quarterly earnings*, Working Paper, University of Washington.

Burgstahler, D and I Dichev (1997), 'Earnings management to avoid earnings decreases and losses', *Journal of Accounting and Economics* Vol. 24(1), pp.99-126.

Burgstahler, D and M Eames (2003), 'Earnings management to avoid losses and earnings decreases: are analysts fooled?', *Contemporary Accounting Research*, Vol.20(2), pp.253-294.

Burgstahler, D and M Eames (1998), *Management of earnings and analyst forecasts*, Working Paper, University of Washington and Santa Clara University.

Byington, J R and S G Sutton (1991), 'The self-regulating profession: An analysis of the political monopoly tendencies of the audit profession', *Critical Perspectives on Accounting*, Vol.2(4), pp.315-330.

Cahill, E (2000), *Tax evasion and DIRT: Breakdowns in corporate governance, auditor objectivity, and ethical behaviour?*, Paper presented at the annual conference of the Irish Accounting and Finance Association, Dublin Institute of Technology, 12th May.

Canning, M and D Gwilliam (1999), 'Non-audit services and auditor independence: Some evidence from Ireland', *The European Accounting Review*, Vol.8(3), pp.401-419.

Canning, M and B O'Dwyer (2001), 'Professional Accounting Bodies' Disciplinary Procedures: Accountable, Transparent and in the Public Interest', *The European Accounting Review*, Vol.10(4), pp.725-749.

Canning, M and B. O'Dwyer (2003), 'A critique of the descriptive power of the private interest model of professional accounting ethics: An examination over time in the Irish context', *Accounting, Auditing & Accountability Journal*, February, Vol.16(2), pp.159-185.

Carcello, J V, D R Hermanson and H F Huss (1996), 'Inappropriate audit partner behavior: Views of partners and senior managers', *Behavioral Research in Accounting*, Vol.8 (supplement), pp.245-268.

Carnegie, G D and J R Edwards (2001), 'The construction of the professional accountant: The case of the Incorporated Institute of Accountants, Victoria (1886)', *Accounting, Organizations and Society*, Vol.26(4/5), pp.301-325.

CGAA (Co-Ordinating Group on Audit and Accounting Issues) (2003), *Final Report to the Secretary of State for trade and Industry and the Chancellor of the Exchequer*, 29 January.

Chandler, R and J R Edwards (1996), 'Recurring issues in auditing: back to the future?', *Accounting, Auditing & Accountability Journal*, Vol.9(2), pp.4-29.

Chaney, P K, D C Jeter and S P Erickson (2003), 'The impact on the market for auditor services of aggressive competition by auditors', *Journal of Accounting and Public Policy*, Vol.22(6), pp.487-516.

Chatfield, M (1978), *The English View of Accountants Duties and Responsibilities 1881-1902*, Arno Press, New York, ppviv + 160.

Chonko L B and S D Hunt (1985), 'Ethics and marketing management: An empirical examination', *Journal of Business Research*, Vol.13(4), pp.339-359.

Chua, W F (1986), 'Radical development in accounting thought', *The Accounting Review*, Vol.61(4), pp.601-632.

Chua W F and C Poullaos (1998), 'The dynamics of 'closure' amidst the construction of market profession, empire and nationhood: An historical analysis of an Australian accounting association, 1886 – 1903', *Accounting, Organizations and Society*, Vol.23(2), pp.155-187

Chua, W F and C Poullaos (1993), 'Rethinking the profession-state dynamic: The case of the Victorian Charter attempt', *Accounting, Organizations and Society*, Vol.18(7/8), pp.691-728.

Chung, H and S Kallapur (2003), 'Client Importance, Non-Audit Services, and Abnormal Accruals', *The Accounting Review*, Vol.78(4), pp.931-955.

Citron, D B (2003), 'The UK's framework approach to auditor independence and the commercialization of the accounting profession', *Accounting, Auditing & Accountability Journal*, February, Vol.16(2), pp.244-274.

Clarke, F, G Dean and K Oliver (2003) *Corporate Collapse: Accounting Regulatory and Ethical Failure*, Cambridge University Press.

Clarke, F, G Dean and K Oliver (1997), *Corporate Collapse: Regulatory, Accounting and Ethical Failure*, Cambridge University Press.

Clikeman, P M, M A Geiger and B T O'Connell (2001a), 'Student perceptions of earnings management: The effects of national origin and gender', *Teaching Business Ethics*, Vol.5(4), pp389-410.

Clikeman, P M, B N Schwartz and M H Lathan (2001b), 'The effect of the 150-hour requirement on new accountants' professional commitment, ethical orientation and professionalism', *Critical Perspective on Accounting*, Vol.12(5), pp.627-645.

Coffee J C (2002), *Understanding Enron: It's about the gatekeepers, Stupid*, Columbia Law & Economics Working Paper No. 207, Available at http://papers.ssrn.com/sol3/papers.cfm?abstract_id=325240.

Cohen J R, L W Pant and D J Sharp (1995), 'An exploratory examination of international differences in auditors' ethical perceptions', *Behavioral Research in Accounting*, Vol.7, pp.37-64.

Cohen, J R, L W Pant and D J Sharp (1993), 'Culture-based ethical conflicts confronting multinational accounting firms', *Accounting Horizons*, Vol.7(3), pp.1-13.

Cook, E and T Kelley (1991), 'An international comparison of audit time-budget pressures: The United States and New Zealand', *The Woman CPA*, (Spring), pp.25-30.

Cooper, D J (2001), *Accounting, Professions and Regulation: Bringing accounting firms in*, Paper presented at the Accounting, Organizations and Society 25th anniversary conference, Oxford, UK.

Copeland J (2003), *Post-Enron challenges for the auditing profession*, Vital Speeches of the Day, April 1, Vol.69(12), pp. 360-364.

Cottell, P J jnr, and T M Perlin (1990), *Accounting Ethics: A practical guide for professionals*, Westport, CT: Quorum Books.

Craig, R J and J H Amernic (2004), 'Enron discourse: The rhetoric of a resilient capitalism', *Critical Perspectives on Accounting*, Vol.15(5/6), pp.813-851.

Crasswell, A, D J Stokes and J Laughton (2002), 'Auditor independence and fee dependence', *Journal of Accounting and Economics*, Vol.33(2), pp.253-275.

Cullinan, C P and S G Sutton (2002), 'Defrauding the public interest: A critical examination of reengineered audit processes and the likelihood of detecting fraud', *Critical Perspectives on Accounting*, Vol.13(3), pp.297-310.

Dalton, T and T Kelley (1997), 'A comparison of dysfunctional behaviors by tax accountants and auditors under time budget pressure', *Advances in Accounting*, Vol.15, pp.193-208.

Daly, B A and D K Schuler (1998), 'Redefining a Certified Public Accounting firm', *Accounting, Organizations and Society*, Vol.23(5/6), pp.549-567.

D'Aquila, J M (2001), 'Financial accountants' perceptions of management's ethical standards', *Journal of Business Ethics*, Vol.31(3), pp.233-244.

Dean, G, F Clarke and P Wolnizer (2002), 'Auditor Independence Reforms – Recycled Ideas', Editorial, *Abacus*, Vol.38(2), pp.i-vi.

Dechow, P M and D J Skinner (2000), 'Earnings management: Reconciling the views of accounting academics, practitioners, and regulators', *Accounting Horizons*, Vol.14(2), pp.235-250.

Dechow, P M, R G Sloan and A P Sweeney (1996), 'Causes and consequences of earnings manipulation: an analysis of firms subject to enforcement actions by the SEC', *Contemporary Accounting Research*, Vol.13(1), pp.1-36.

DeFond M L and J R Francis (2005), 'Audit Research after Sarbanes-Oxley', *Auditing: A Journal of Practice & Theory*, Vol.24 (Supplement), pp.5-30.

DeFond M L, K Raghunandan and K R Subramanyam (2002), 'Do Non-audit Service Fees Impair Auditor Independence? Evidence from Going Concern Audit Opinions', *Journal of Accounting Research*, Vol. 40(4), pp.1247–1274.

DeGeorge, F, J Patel and R Zeckhauser (1999), 'Earnings management to exceed thresholds', *Journal of Business*, Vol.72(1), pp.1-33.

Dewing, I P and O Russell (2003), 'Post-Enron developments in UK audit and corporate governance regulation', *Journal of financial regulation and compliance*, Vol.11(4), pp.309-322

Dezalay, Y (1997), 'Accountants as 'new guard dogs' of capitalism: Stereotype or research agenda?, *Accounting Organizations and Society*, Vol.22(8), pp.825 - 829.

DeZoort, F T and A T Lord (1997), 'A review and synthesis of pressure effects research in accounting', *Journal of Accounting Literature*, Vol.16, pp.28-85

Dirsmith, M W and M A Covaleski (1985), 'Informal communications, nonformal communications and mentoring in public accounting firms', *Accounting, Organizations and Society*, Vol.10(2), pp.149-169.

Douglas, P C, R A Davidson and B N Schwartz (2001), 'The Effects of Organizational Ethical orientation on Accountants' *Ethical Judgements*', *Journal of Business Ethics*, Vol.34(2), pp.101-121.

Duff, A (1988), 'Up to the task', *CA Magazine*, p.3.

Dugan, I J (2002), 'Auditing Old-Timers recall when the bottom line was their own prestige', *The Wall Street Journal Europe*, 16 July.

Dunn, J and M Stewart (1999), 'Resignation or abdication - the credibility of auditor resignation statements', *Accounting Forum*, March, Vol.23(1), pp.35-57.

Duska R. (2005), 'The good auditor – Skeptic or Wealth accumulator? Ethical lessons learned from the Arthur Andersen debacle', *Journal of Business Ethics*, Vol.57(1), pp.17-29.

Dwyer P G and R W Roberts (2004), 'Known by the company they keep: a study of political campaign contributions made by the United States public accounting profession', *Critical Perspectives on Accounting*, Vol.15(6/7), pp.865–883.

Dye, R A (1988), 'Earnings management in an overlapping generations model', *Journal of Accounting Research*, Vol.28(2), pp.195-236.

Economist, 1990, *Blowing the whistle on accountancy*, December 22: p.17.

Edwards, J D (1987), 'The American Institute of Certified Public Accountants: A century of Progress and Commitment to the Accountancy Profession', *The Accounting Historians Journal*, Vol.14(1), pp.111-121.

Edwards, J R (2003), *Towards better describing and locating within commerce and society the 'Public Accountant' in England prior to organisational fusion*, Paper presented at University of Sydney Accounting Foundation Research Seminar Series, 19 March.

Edwards, J R (2001), 'Accounting regulation and the professionalization process: An historical essay concerning the significance of P H Abbott', *Critical Perspectives on Accounting*, Vol.12(6), pp.675-696.

Elias, R Z (2002), 'Determinants of earnings management ethics among accountants', *Journal of Business Ethics*, Vol.40(1), pp.33-45.

Elliott, R K (1998), 'Assurance services and the audit heritage: What's new and what's rooted in the past', *The CPA Journal*, June, pp.40-47.

Eynon, G, N Thorley Hill and K T Stevens (1997), 'Factors that influence the Moral Reasoning Abilities of Accountants: Implications for universities and the profession', *Journal of Business Ethics*, Vol.16(12/13), pp.1297-1309.

Eynon, G, N Thorley Hill, K T Stevens and Clarke, P (1996), 'An International Comparison of Ethical Reasoning Abilities: Accounting Students From Ireland and The United States', *Journal of Accounting Education*, Vol.14(4), pp.477-492.

Everett, J, D Green and D Neu (2005), 'Independence, objectivity and the Canadian CA profession', *Critical Perspectives on Accounting*, Vol.16(4), pp.415-440.

Everett, J (2002), *Independence, Objectivity and the Canadian CA Profession*, Paper presented at UNSW School of Accounting Research Seminar Series, 20 September.

Fearnley, S, V A Beattie and R Brandt (2005), 'Auditor Independence and Audit Risk: A reconceptualisation', *Journal of International Accounting Research*, Vol.4(1), pp.39-71.

Fearnley, S, T Hines, K McBride and R Brandt (2002) 'The impact of the Financial Reporting Review Panel on aspects of the independence of auditors and their attitudes to compliance in the UK', *British Accounting Review*, Vol.34(2), pp.109-139.

Finn D W, L B Chonko and S D Hunt (1988), 'Ethical problems in public accounting: The view from the top', *Journal of Business Ethics*, July, Vol.7(8), pp.605-615.

Firth, M (1997), 'The provision of non-audit services by accounting firms to their audit clients', *Contemporary Accounting Research*, Summer, Vol.14(2), pp.1-21.

Fischer, M and K Rosenzweig (1995), 'Attitudes of Students and Accounting Practitioners Concerning the Ethical Acceptability of Earnings Management', *Journal of Business Ethics*, Vol.14(6), pp.433-444.

Fisher, J, S Gunz and J McCutcheon (2001), 'Private/Public Interest and the Enforcement of a Code of professional Conduct', *Journal of Business Ethics*, Vol.31(3), pp.191-207.

Fisher, C and A Lovell (2000), *Accountants' responses to ethical issues at work*, London: CIMA.

Flanigan, M A, R H Tondkar and E N Coffman (1994), 'The comparative development of the accounting profession in England, the United States, and Australia: a sociological interpretation', *Advances in International Accounting*, Vol.6, pp.295-316.

Fogarty. T J (2000), 'Socialization and organizational outcomes in large public accounting firms', *Journal of Managerial Issues*, Vol.12(1), pp.13-33.

Fogarty, T (1996), 'The imagery and reality of peer review in the US: Insights from institutional theory', *Accounting, Organizations and Society*, Vol.21(2/3), pp.243-267.

Fogarty, T (1992), 'Organizational Socialization in Public Accounting Firms: A Theoretical Framework and Agenda for Future Research', *Accounting, Organizations and Society*, Vol.17(2), pp.129-149.

Fogarty, T J, L J Zucca, N Meonske and D P Kirch (1997), 'Proactive practice review: A critical case study of accounting regulation that never was', *Critical Perspectives on Accounting*, Vol.8(3), pp.167-187.

Fogarty T, J Heian and D Knutson (1991), 'The rationality of doing nothing: Auditors' responses to legal liability in an institutionalized environment', *Critical Perspectives on Accounting*, Vol.2, pp.201-226.

Francis, J R (1990), 'After Virtue? Accounting as a Moral and Discursive practice', *Accounting, Auditing and Accountability Journal*, Vol.3(3), pp.5-17.

Frankel, M S (1989), 'Professional Codes: Why, How and with What impact?', *Journal of Business Ethics*, Vol.8(2/3), pp.109-115.

Frankel, R, M Johnson and K Nelson (2002), 'The relationship between auditor's fees for non-audit services and earnings management', *The Accounting Review*, Vol.77(Supplement), pp.71-105.

Friedland J (2004), 'Time to end the Big Four accounting cartel', *International Journal of Disclosure and Governance*, Vol.1(3), pp.211-213.

Fuerman, R D (2004), 'Accountable Accountants', *Critical Perspectives on Accounting*, Vol.15(5/6), pp.911-926.

Gaa, J (2004), 'Introduction: Special Issue on Accounting Ethics', *Business Ethics Quarterly*, Vol.14(3), pp.349-354.

Gaa, J C (1994), *The Ethical Foundations of Public Accounting*, Research Monograph No. 22, CGA – Canada Research Foundation, Certified General Accountants' Association of Canada.

Gaa, J C (1991), 'The expectations game: Regulation of auditors by government and the profession', *Critical Perspectives on Accounting*, Vol.2(1), pp.83-107.

Gendron, Y (2002), 'On the role of the organization in auditors' client-acceptance decisions', *Accounting, Organizations and Society*, Vol.27(7), pp.659-684.

Gendron, Y (2001), 'The difficult client-acceptance decision in Canadian audit firms: A field investigation', *Contemporary Accounting Research*, Vol.18(2), pp.283-310.

Gendron, Y (2000), 'Openness to context-based research: The gulf between the claims and actions of Big Six firms in the USA', *Accounting, Auditing and Accountability Journal*, Vol.13(2), pp.175-196.

Gilfedder, D and C Ó hÓgartaigh, (1998) 'The grasshopper and the great cattle: Participation and non-participation in the ASB's standard-setting process', *Journal of Management and Governance*, Vol.2(3), pp.287-296.

Gillett, P R. and N Uddin (2005), 'CFO Intentions of Fraudulent Financial Reporting', *Auditing: A Journal of Practice & Theory*, Vol.24(1), pp.55-75.

Goode, W J (1957) 'Community within a community: the professions' *American Sociological Review*, Vol.22(2), pp.194–200.

Grant, T, C M Jnr Depree and G H Grant (2000), 'Earnings management and the abuse of materiality', *Journal of Accountancy*, September, pp.41-44.

Gray, S (2004), 'Companies try New Mix on Boards', *Wall Street Journal Europe*, January 8.

Grey, C (1998), 'On being a professional in a 'Big Six' Firm', *Accounting, Organizations and Society*, Vol.23(5/6), pp.569-587.

Greenwood, E (1966), *The elements of professionalization* in Vollmer H M and D L Mills (Eds) Professionalization, Englewood Cliffs, NJ, Prentice Hall.

Gunz, H P, S Gunz and J C McCutcheon (2002), 'Organizational influences on approaches to ethical decisions by professionals: The case of public accountants', *Administrative Sciences Association of Canada*, March, Vol.19(1), pp.76-91.

Gunz, S and J McCutcheon (1991), 'Some unresolved ethical issues in auditing', *Journal of Business Ethics*, Vol.10(10), pp.777-785.

Hamilton, S (2004), 'Back to Basics: Summer School perspectives', *CA Magazine*, July, pp.35-36.

Hanlon, G (1997), 'Commercialising the service class and economic restructuring - A response to my critics', *Accounting, Organizations and Society*, Vol.22(8), pp.843 - 855.

Hanlon, G (1994), *The Commercialization of Accountancy: Flexible Accumulation and the Transformation of the Service Class*, Macmillan, London.

Haskell, L (1984), *The Authority of Experts*, Indiana University Press, Bloomington.

Hayward, J (2003), *Thinking not ticking: Bringing competition to the public interest audit*, Centre for the Study of Financial Innovation, Kent.

Healy, P M and J M Wahlen (1999), 'A review of the earnings management literature and its implications for standard-setting', *Accounting Horizons*, December, Vol.3(4), pp.365-383.

Hendrickson, H (1998), 'Relevant financial reporting questions not asked by the accounting profession', *Critical Perspectives on Accounting*, Vol.9(5), pp.489-505.

Hermanson D R and P D Lapides (2003), 'Make your work more visible – So it can have impact', *The Auditors' Report*, Vol.27(1), pp.6-9.

Herrbach, O (2002), *(Maybe) not that dysfunctional after all: Audit quality reduction behaviours and the evolution of auditing methods*, Paper presented at the 25th EAA Conference, Copenhagen, 25-27 April, 2002.

Herron, T L and D L Gilbertson (2004), 'Ethical principles Vs. ethical rules: The moderating effect of moral development on audit independence judgements', *Business Ethics Quarterly*, Vol.14(3), pp.499-523.

Higgins, T G and W E Olson (1972), 'Restating the ethics code: A decision for the times', *Journal of Accountancy*, March, pp.34-39.

Higgs-Kleyn, N and D Kapelianis (1999), 'The role of professional codes in regulating ethical conduct', *Journal of Business Ethics*, Vol.19(4), pp.363-374.

Hill, N T, S W Shelton, and K T Stevens (2002), 'Corporate Lobbying Behaviour on Accounting for Stock-Based Compensation: Venue and Format Choices', *Abacus*, Vol.38(1), pp.78-90.

Hodge, F D (2003), 'Investors' perceptions of earnings quality, auditor independence, and the usefulness of audited financial information', *Accounting Horizons*, Vol.17 (Supplement), pp.37-48.

Hooks, K L (1991), 'Professionalism and self-interest: A critical view of the expectations gap', *Critical Perspectives on Accounting*, Vol.3(2), pp.109-136.

Hopwood, A G (1998), 'Exploring the modern audit firm', *Accounting, Organizations and Society*, Vol.23(5/6), pp.515-516.

Howitt, H (1966), *The History of the Institute of Chartered Accountants in England and Wales 1880-1965 and of its Founder Accountancy Bodies 1870 – 1880*, Heinemann, London.

Hume, E C, E R Larkins and G Iyer (1999), 'On compliance with ethical standards in tax return preparation', *Journal of Business Ethics*, Vol.18(2), pp.229-238.

Humphrey, C, P Moizer and S Turley (1992), 'The Audit Expectations Gap – Plus ça Change, Plus c'est la meme Chose?' *Critical Perspectives on Accounting*, Vol.3(2), pp.217-238.

Humphrey, C G, and P Moizer (1991), 'From techniques to ideologies: An alternative perspective on the audit function' *Critical Perspectives on Accounting*, Vol.1(3), pp.137-162.

Hunt, S and S Vitell (1991), 'The general theory of marketing ethics: a retrospective and revision' in Smith N C and J A Guelch (Eds), *Ethics in Marketing*, Irwin, Homewood Il, pp.775-784.

Hunt, S D and S J Vitell (1986), 'A general theory of marketing ethics', *Journal of Macromarketing*, pp.5-16.

Hussey, R (1999), 'The familiarity threat and auditor independence', *Corporate Governance*, Vol.7(2), pp.190-197.

ICAI (Institute of Chartered Accountants in Ireland), (2003), *Ethical Guide for Members*, ICAI, Dublin and Belfast.

ICAS (Institute of Chartered Accountants of Scotland) (2006), *Principles Not Rules: A Question of Judgement*, ICAS, Edinburgh.

ICAS (Institute of Chartered Accountants of Scotland) (2004), *Taking Ethics to Heart* (Eds Helliar, C and Bebbington, J), A Discussion Document by the Research Committee of ICAS, Edinburgh.

Irish Times, Anonymous (2005), *KPMG admits to fraud schemes in US*, Irish Times, August 30.

Jackson, B and V Milliron (1986), 'Tax compliance research: Findings, problems and prospects', *Journal of Accounting Literature*, Vol.5, pp.125-166.

Jeffrey, C, W Dilla and N Westherholt (2004), 'The impact of ethical development and cultural constructs on auditor judgements: A study of auditors in Taiwan', *Business Ethics Quarterly*, Vol.14(3), pp.553-579.

Johnstone, K M, M H Sutton and T D Warfield (2001), 'Antecedents and Consequences of Independence risk: Framework for Analysis', *Accounting Horizons*, Vol.15(1), pp.1-18.

Jones, T (1991), 'Ethical decision making by individuals in organizations: An issue-contingent model', *Academy of Management Review*, Vol.16(2), pp.366-395.

Jones, J, D W Massey and L Thorne (2003), 'Auditors' Ethical Reasoning: Insights from past research and implications for the future', *Journal of Accounting Literature*, Vol.22, pp.45-103.

Jones, D G B, A J Richardson and T Shearer (2000), 'Truth and the evolution of the professions: A comparative study of 'truth in advertising' and 'true and fair' financial statements in North America during the Progressive Era', *Journal of Macromarketing*, June, Vol.20(1), pp.23-35.

Joplin, J P (1914), 'Ethics of Accountancy', *Journal of Accountancy*, March, pp.187-196.

Kaplan, S E (2001), 'Further evidence on the ethics of managing earnings: an examination of the ethically related judgements of shareholders and non-shareholders', *Journal of Accounting and Public Policy*, Vol.20(1), pp.27-44.

Karcher, J N (1996), 'Auditors' ability to discern the presence of ethical problems', *Journal of Business Ethics*, Vol.15(10), pp.1033-1050.

Karnes A, J Sterner, R Welker and F Wu (1990), 'A bi-cultural comparison of accountants' perceptions of unethical business practices', *Accounting, Auditing & Accountability Journal*, Vol.3(3), pp.45-64.

Kedslie, M J M (1990), *Firm Foundations: The Development of Professional Accounting in Scotland 1850 – 1900*, Hull University Press.

Keena, C (2002), *Auditor advised clients on Ansbacher*, The Irish Times. 12 July.

Kelley, T and L Margheim (1990), 'The impact of time budget pressure, personality, and leadership variables on dysfunctional auditor behavior', *Auditing: A Journal of Practice & Theory*, Vol.9 (Fall), pp.21-42.

Kelley, T and L Margheim (1987), 'The effect of audit billing arrangement on underreporting of time and audit quality reduction acts', *Advances in Accounting*, Vol.5, pp.221-233.

Kelley, T and R E Seiler (1982), 'Auditor stress and time budgets', *The CPA Journal*, December: pp.24-34.

Kirkham L M and A Loft (1993), 'Gender and the construction of the professional accountant', *Accounting, Organizations and Society*, Vol.18(6), pp.507-558.

Kleinman, G, D Palmon and A Anandarajan (1998), 'Auditor independence: A synthesis of theory and empirical research', *Research in Accounting Regulation*, Vol.12, pp.3-42.

Larson, M S (1977), *The Rise of Professionalism: A Sociological Analysis*, University of California Press, Berkeley.

Latham, C K and F A Jacobs (2000), 'Monitoring and incentive factors influencing misleading disclosures', *Journal of Managerial Issues,* Vol.12(2), pp.169-187.

Lee, T A (2002), 'UK immigrants and the foundation of the US public accountancy profession', *Accounting, Business & Financial History*, Vol.12(1), pp.73-95.

Lee, T A (2001), 'US public accountancy firms and the recruitment of UK immigrants: 1850-1914', *Accounting, Auditing & Accountability Journal*, Vol.14(5), pp.537-565.

Lee, T A (1997), 'The influence of Scottish Accountants in the US: The early case of the Society of Accountants in Edinburgh', *The Accounting Historians Journal*, Vol.24(1), pp.117-141.

Lee, T (1995), 'The professionalization of accountancy: A history of protecting the public interest in a self-interested way', *Accounting, Auditing & Accountability Journal*, April 1, Vol.8(4), pp. 48-69.

Lee, T (1994), 'Financial Reporting Quality Labels: The social construction of the audit profession and the expectations gap', *Accounting, Auditing & Accountability Journal*, Vol.7(2), pp.30-49.

Lee, T A (1991), 'A Review Essay: Professional Foundations and Theories of Professional Behavior', *The Accounting Historians Journal*, Vol.18(2), pp.193-203.

Leung, P and B J Cooper (1995), 'Ethical Dilemmas in Accountancy Practice', *Australian Accountant*, May, pp.28-33.

Levitt A (2002), *Take on the Street*, Pantheon Books, New York.

Levitt, A (1998), 'The Numbers game', *The CPA Journal*, December, pp.15-19.

Liu, C and S Ryan (1995), 'The effect of loan portfolio composition on the market reaction to and anticipation of loan loss provisions', *Journal of Accounting Research*, Vol.33(1) (Spring), pp.77-94.

Loomis, C J (1999), 'Lies, damned lies, and managed earnings', *Fortune*, Vol.140(3), pp.74-83.

Lord A T and F T DeZoort (2001), 'The impact of commitment and moral reasoning on auditors' responses to social influence pressure', *Accounting, Organizations and Society*, Vol.26(3), pp.215-235.

Lovell, A (2005), *Ethics in Business: A Literature Review*, The Institute of Chartered Accountants of Scotland, Edinburgh.

Lovell, A (1995), 'Moral reasoning and moral atmosphere in the domain of accounting', *Accounting, Auditing & Accountability Journal,* Vol.8(3), pp.60-80.

Lucci, J P (2003), 'New York revises its ethics rules to permit limited MDPs: A critical analysis of the New York approach, the future of the MDP debate after Enron, and recommendations for other jurisdictions', *Fordham Journal of Corporate and Financial Law*, Vol.8(1), pp.151 – 200.

Luehlfing, M S (1995), 'The politics of self-imposed regulations - has a new day dawned?', *Accounting Horizons*, Vol.9(2), pp.68-76.

Luscombe N (1985), 'Carving with Caution', *CA Magazine*, p.3.

MacDonald, K M (1989), 'Building respectability', *Sociology*, Vol.23(1), pp.55-80.

MacDonald K M (1985a), 'Social closure and Occupational registration', *Sociology*, Vol.19(4), pp.541-556.

MacDonald K M (1985b), *The Sociology of the Professions*, Sage Publications, London.

MacDonald K M (1984), 'Professional Formation: The case of Scottish Accountants', *The British Journal of Sociology*, Vol.35(2), pp.174-189.

MacDonald, C, M McDonald and W Norman (2002), 'Charitable conflicts of interest', *Journal of Business Ethics*, Vol.39(1/2), pp.67-74.

McBarnet, D and C Whelan (1999), *Creative Accounting and the Cross-eyed Javelin Thrower*, Chichester, Wiley.

McDaniel, L S (1990), 'The effects of time pressure and audit program structure on audit performance', *Journal of Accounting Research*, Vol.28(2), pp.267-285.

McEnroe, J E and S C Martens (2001), 'Auditors' and Investors' perceptions of the expectations gap', *Accounting Horizons*, Vol.15(4), pp.345-358.

McKee, A J, P F Williams and K B Frazier (1991), 'A case study of accounting firm lobbying: Advice or consent', *Critical Perspectives on Accounting*, Vol.2(3), pp.273-294.

McMillan, K P (2004), 'Trust and virtues: A solution to the accounting scandals?', *Critical Perspectives on Accounting*, Vol.15(5/6), pp.943-953.

McMillan K P (1999), The Institute of Accounts: a community of the competent', *Accounting, Business & Financial History*, Vol.9(1), pp.7-28.

McNair, C J (1991), 'Proper compromises: The management control dilemma in public accounting and its impact on auditor behaviour', *Accounting, Organizations and Society*, Vol.16(7), pp.635-653.

McNichols, M F (2000), 'Research design issues in earnings management studies', *Journal of Accounting and Public Policy*, Vol.19(4/5), pp.313-345.

McPhail, K (2006), *Ethics and the Individual Professional Accountant: A Literature Review*, The Institute of Chartered Accountants of Scotland, Edinburgh.

McPhail, K (2003), 'Relocating accounting and business ethics: Reflections on a business ethics retreat in Scotland's National Park', *The British Accounting Review*, Vol.35(4), pp.349-366.

McPhail, K and R Gray (1996), *Not developing ethical maturity in accounting education: Hegemony, dissonance, and homogeneity in accounting students' world views*, Working paper, Draft 3A, University of Dundee, The Centre for Social and Environmental Research.

Magill, H and G Previts (1991), *CPA Professional Responsibilities: An introduction*, Cincinnati, South-Western Publishing Co.

Malone, C F and R W Roberts (1996), 'Factors associated with the incidence of reduced audit quality behaviors', *Auditing: A Journal of Practice & Theory*, Vol.15(2), pp.49-64.

Margheim, L and K Pany (1986), 'Quality control, premature sign-off, and under-reporting of time: some empirical findings', *Auditing: A Journal of Practice & Theory*, Vol.5(2), pp.50-63.

Mautz, R K (1988), 'Public Accounting: Which kind of professionalism?', *Accounting Horizons*, September, Vol.2(3), pp.121-125.

Mayhew B W and J E Pike (2004), 'Does Investor Selection of Auditors Enhance Auditor Independence?', *Accounting Review*, Vol.79(3), pp.797-822.

Mayper, A G, R J Pavur, B D Merino and W Hoops (2005), 'The Impact of Accounting Education on Ethical Values: An Institutional Perspective', *Accounting in the Public Interest,* Vol.5, pp.32-55.

Meehan, M (1997/8), 'State bank bunkum and the 4 billion dollar blowout', *Accounting Forum*, Vol.21(3/4), pp.339-360.

Merchant K A (1987), *Fraudulent and Questionable Financial Reporting: A Corporate Perspective*, Morristown, NJ. Financial Executives' Research Foundation.

Merchant, K A and J Rockness (1994), 'The ethics of managing earnings: An empirical investigation', *Journal of Accounting and Public Policy*, Vol.13(1), pp.79-95.

Merino, B D and A G Mayper (2001), 'Securities legislation and the accounting profession in the 1930s: The rhetoric and reality of the American dream', *Critical Perspectives on Accounting*, Vol.12(4), pp.501-525.

Miller, T (1992), 'Do we need to consider the individual auditor when discussing auditor independence?' *Accounting, Auditing & Accountability Journal*, Vol.5(1), pp.74-84.

Mills, S K and M S Bettner (1992), 'Ritual and Conflict in the Audit Profession', *Critical Perspectives on Accounting*, Vol.3(2), pp.185-200.

Mitchell, A and P Sikka (1993), 'Accounting for change: The institutions of accountancy', *Critical Perspectives on Accounting*, Vol.4(1), pp.29-52.

Mitchell, A, P Sikka and H Willmott (1998), 'Sweeping it under the carpet: The role of accountancy firms in moneylaundering', *Accounting, Organizations and Society*, Vol.23(5/6), pp.589-607.

Mitchell, A, P Sikka, P Arnold, C Cooper and H Willmott (2000), *The BCCI Cover-up*, Association for Accounting and Business affairs, Basildon.

Mitchell, A, T Puxty, P Sikka and H Willmott (1994), 'Ethical statements as smokescreens for sectional interests: the case of the UK accountancy profession', *Journal of Business Ethics*, Vol.13(1), pp.39-51.

Moizer, P (1995), 'An Ethical Approach to the Choices Faced by Auditors', *Critical Perspectives on Accounting*, Vol.6(5), pp.415-431.

Moriarity, S (2000), 'Trends in ethical sanctions within the accounting profession', *Accounting Horizons*, December, Vol.14(4), pp.427-439.

Morris T and L Empson (1998), 'Organisation and expertise: An exploration of knowledge bases and the management of accounting and consulting firms', *Accounting, Organizations and Society*, Vol.23(5/6), pp.609-624.

Murphy G (1986), 'A chronology of the development of corporate financial reporting in Canada: 1850 – 1983', *The Accounting Historians Journal*, Vol.13, pp.31-61.

Myers J, L Myers and T Omer (2003), 'Exploring the term of auditor-client relationship and the quality of earnings: A case for mandatory auditor rotation?', *The Accounting Review*, Vol.78(3), pp.779-799.

National Commission on Fraudulent Financial Reporting (1987), *Report of the national commission on fraudulent financial reporting*, Washington, DC: NCFFR.

Nelson, M W, J A Elliott and R L Tarpley (2002), 'Evidence from auditors about managers' and auditors' earnings management decisions', *The Accounting Review*, Vol.77 (Supplement), pp.175-202.

Neu, D (1991), 'Trust, Impression Management and the Public Accounting Profession', *Critical Perspectives on Accounting*, Vol.2(3), pp.295-313.

Neu, D, C Friesen and J Everett (2003), 'The changing internal market for ethical discourses in the Canadian CA profession', *Accounting, Auditing & Accountability Journal*, Vol.16(1), pp.70-103.

Neu, D and L Saleem (1996), 'The Institute of Chartered Accountants of Ontario (ICAO) and the emergence of ethical codes', *The Accounting Historians Journal*, Vol.23(2), pp.35-68.

Neu, D and R T'aerien (2000), 'Remembering the past: Ethics and the Canadian Chartered Accounting Profession, 1911 – 1925', *Critical Perspectives on Accounting*, Vol.11(2), pp.193-212.

Newman, D P (1981), 'An investigation of the distribution of power in the APB and FASB', *Journal of Accounting Research*, Vol.19(1), pp.247-262.

Nieschwietz, R J, J J Jr Schultz and M F Zimbelman (2000), 'Empirical research on external auditors' detection of financial statement fraud', *Journal of Accounting Literature*, Vol.19, pp.190–246.

O'Connell B T (2004), 'Enron. Con: 'He that filches from me my good name … makes me poor indeed" *Critical Perspectives on Accounting*, Vol.15(6/7), pp.733-749.

Otley, D and B J Pierce (1996a), 'The operation of control systems in large audit firms: An empirical investigation', *Auditing: A Journal of Practice & Theory*, Vol.15 (Fall), pp.65-84.

Otley, D and B J Pierce (1996b), 'Auditor time budget pressure: consequences and antecedents', *Accounting, Auditing & Accountability Journa1*, Vol.9 (Spring), pp.31-58.

Ouchi ,W G (1980), 'Markets, Bureaucracies and Clans', *Administrative Science Quarterly*, Vol.25(1), pp.129-141.

Ouchi, W G (1979), 'A conceptual framework for the design of organizational control mechanisms', *Management Science*, Vol.25(9), pp.833-848.

Parfet W U (2000), 'Accounting subjectivity and earnings management: A preparer perspective', *Accounting Horizons*, Vol.14(4), pp.481-488.

Parker, L D (1994), 'Professional Accounting Body Ethics: In search of the Private Interest', *Accounting Organizations and Society*, Vol.19(6), pp.507-525.

Paterson, R (2004), 'Back to Basics: Summer School perspectives', *CA Magazine*, July p.35.

Peace, R (2006), 'Accountants and a religious covenant with the public', *Critical Perspectives on Accounting*, Vol.17(6), pp.781-797.

Peppas, S C and G J Peppas (2000), 'Business ethics in the European Union: a study of Greek attitudes', *Management Decision*, Vol.38(6), pp.369-376.

Phiddian, R (1996), 'Political arithmetick: Accounting for irony in Swift's A Modest Proposal', *Accounting, Auditing & Accountability Journal*, Vol. 9(5), pp.71-83.

Phillips, C (2001) *Socrates Café: A fresh Taste of Philosophy*. New York, NY. W W Norton.

Pierce, A (2003), 'Elan Corporation: A case study in corporate obfuscation', *Corporate Governance International*, Vol.6(1), pp.5-23.

Pierce, B and B Sweeney (2003), 'Auditor responses to cost controls', *Irish Accounting Review*, Vol.10(1), pp.45-68.

Pierce, B and B Sweeney (2004), 'Cost-Quality conflict in audit firms: An empirical investigation', *European Accounting Review*, Vol.13(3), pp.415-441.

Pierce, B and B Sweeney (2005), 'Management Control in audit firms – Partners' perspectives', *Management Accounting Research*, Vol.16(3), pp.340-370.

Pincus, K V (2000), 'The role of rules in accounting: do rules guide us to the right path or to the path of least resistance?', *Research on Accounting Ethics*, Vol.6, pp.293-258.

Ponemon, L A (1993), 'Can ethics be taught in Accounting', *Journal of Accounting, Education*, Vol.11(2), pp.185-209.

Ponemon, L A (1992), 'Ethical Reasoning and Selection-Socialization in Accounting', *Accounting, Organizations and Society*, Vol.17(3/4), pp.239-258.

Ponemon, L A and D R L Gabhart (1990), 'Auditor independence judgements: A cognitive-developmental model and experimental evidence', *Contemporary Accounting Research*, Vol.7(1), pp.227-251.

Ponemon L A and A Glazer, (1990), 'Accounting Education and Ethical Development: The Influence of Liberal Learning on Students and Alumni in Accounting Practice', *Issues in Accounting Education*, Vol.5(2), pp.195-208.

Portwood D and A Fielding (1981), 'Privilege and the Professions', *Sociological Review*, Vol.29(4), pp.749-773.

Power, M K (2003), 'Auditing and the production of legitimacy', *Accounting, Organizations and Society*, Vol.28(4), pp.379-394.

Pratt, J, L C Mohrweis and P Beaulieu (1993), 'The interaction between national and organizational culture in accounting firms: an extension', *Accounting, Organizations and Society*, Vol.18(7/8), pp.621-628.

Preston, A M, D J Cooper, D P Scarbrough and R C Chilton (1995), 'Changes in the Code of Ethics of the U.S. Accounting Profession, 1917 and 1988: The Continual Quest for Legitimation', *Accounting, Organizations and Society*, Vol.20(6), pp.507-546.

Public Oversight Board (1979) *Scope of Services by CPA Firms*. New York, NY: Public Oversight Board.

Puro, M (1985), 'Do large accounting firms collude in the standards-setting process?', *Journal of Accounting, Auditing and Finance*, Vol.8(3), pp.165-177.

Puxty, A, P Sikka and H Willmott (1997), 'Mediating Interests: The Accountancy Bodies' Responses to the McFarlane Report', *Accounting and Business Research*, Vol.27(4), pp.323-340.

Radcliffe, V, D J Cooper and K Robson (1994), 'The management of professional enterprises and regulatory change: British accountancy and the Financial Services Act, 1986', *Accounting, Organizations and Society*, Vol.19(7), pp.601-628.

Raghunandan K, W J Read and J S Whisenant (2003), 'Initial evidence on the association between non-audit fees and restated financial statements', *Accounting Horizons*, Vol.17(3), pp.223-234.

Reinstein, A and J J McMillan (2004), 'The Enron debacle: More than a perfect storm', *Critical Perspectives on Accounting*, Vol.15(5/6), pp.955-970.

Reiter, S (1997), 'The ethics of care and new paradigms for accounting practice', *Accounting, Auditing & Accountability Journal*, Vol.10(3), pp.299-324.

Rest, J (1983), 'Morality' in Flavell, J and E Markman (eds.), *Handbook of Child Psychology*, 4th edition, New York, NY, John Wiley & Sons.

Rest, J, D Narvaez, M Bebeau and S Thoma (1999), 'A Neo Kohlbergian Approach: The DIT and Schema Theory', *Educational Psychology Review*, Vol.11(4), pp.291-324.

Revsine, L (2002), 'Enron: sad but inevitable', *Journal of Accounting and Public Policy*, Vol.21(2), pp.137–145.

Revsine, L (1991), 'The selective financial misrepresentative hypothesis', *Accounting Horizons*, Vol.5(4), pp.16-27.

Reynolds, B (2003), 'It's not over yet', *Accountancy*, March, p.57.

Reynolds, J K, D R Deis and J R Francis (2004), 'Professional Service Fees and Auditor Objectivity', *Auditing: A Journal of Practice & Theory*, March, pp.29-52.

Reynolds, M A (2000), 'Professionalism, ethical codes and the internal auditor: A moral argument', *Journal of Business Ethics*, March, Vol.24(2), pp.115-124.

Rezaee, Z (2005), 'Causes, consequences, and deterrence of financial statement fraud', *Critical Perspectives on Accounting*, Vol.16(3), pp.277-298.

Rhode, J G (1978), *Survey on the influence of selected aspects of the auditor's work environment on the professional performance of certified public accountants,* in The independent auditor's work environment: A survey, CAR Research Study No.4, New York: AICPA.

Richardson, A J (2001), 'The Canadian Audit Market in the first half of the twentieth century', *The Accounting Historians Journal*, Vol.28(2), pp.109-139.

Roberts J and J A Coutts (1992), 'Feminization and Professionalization: A Review of an Emerging Literature on the Development of Accounting in the United Kingdom', *Accounting, Organization and Society*, Vol.17(3/4), pp.379-395.

Roberts, J and M Dietrich (1999), 'Conceptualizing Professionalism: Why economics needs sociology', *The American Journal of Economics and Sociology*, October, Vol.58(4), pp.977-998.

Roberts, R W (2001), 'Commercialism and its impact on the integrity of professional tax services in the United States', *Critical Perspectives on Accounting*, Vol.12(5), pp.589-605.

Roberts, T C (1987), 'The American Association of Public Accountants (1908)', *The Accounting Historians Journal*, Vol.14(2), pp.99-108.

Robinson, D (1999), 'Blurring lines: the future of professional firms', *The National Public Accountant*, August, Vol.44(6), pp.24-27.

Rollins, T P and W G Bremser (1997), 'The SEC's enforcement actions against auditors: an auditor reputation and institutional theory perspective', *Critical Perspectives on Accounting*, Vol.8(3), pp.191-206.

Romeo, G C and L S Kyj (1998), 'The forgotten Accounting Association: The Institute of Account(ant)s', *The Accounting Historians Journal*, Vol.25(1), pp.29-55.

Roy, N (1998), 'Accounting troubles: Management sets the tone', *Financial Executive*, Vol.14, pp.6-7.

Ruland, R G and C K Lindblom (1992), 'Ethics and Disclosure: An Analysis of Conflicting Duties', *Critical Perspectives on Accounting*, Vol.3(3), pp.259-272.

Sawyer, L B (1991), 'Internal Auditing: Practice and Professionalism', *Internal Auditor* (June), pp.38-42.

Schaefer, J and R B Welker (1994), 'Distinguishing characteristics of certified public accountants disciplined for unprofessional behavior', *Journal of Accounting and Public Policy*, Vol.13(2), pp.97–119.

Schipper, K (1989), 'Commentary on Earnings Management', *Accounting Horizons*, Vol.3(4), pp.91-102.

Schuetze, W P (1994), 'A Mountain or a Molehill?', *Accounting Horizons*, Vol.8(1), pp.69-75.

Scofield S B, T J Phillips Jr, and C D Bailey (2004), 'An empirical reanalysis of the selection-socialization hypothesis: a research note', *Accounting, Organizations and Society*, Vol.29(5/6), pp.543-563.

Seal, W and P Vincent-Jones (1997), 'Accounting and trust in the enabling of long-term relations', *Accounting, Auditing & Accountability Journal*, Vol.10(3), pp.406-431.

Shackleton, K (1995), 'Scottish Chartered Accountants: Internal and external political relationships, 1853-1916', *Accounting, Auditing & Accountability Journal*, Vol.8(2), pp.18-46.

Shafer, W E, D J Lowe and T J Fogarty (2002), 'The effects of corporate ownership on Public Accountants' Professionalism and Ethics', *Accounting Horizons*, June, Vol.16(2), pp.109-124.

Shafer, W E, R E Morris and A A Ketchand (2001), 'Effects of personal values on auditors' ethical decisions', *Accounting, Auditing & Accountability Journal*, Vol.14(3), pp.254-277.

Sharma, D S and J Sidhu (2001), 'Professionalism vs Commercialism: The association between non-audit services (NAS) and audit independence', *Journal of Business, Finance and Accounting*, Vol.28(5/6), pp.595-629.

Shaub, M, D Finn and P Munter (1993), 'The effects of auditors' ethical orientation on commitment and ethical sensitivity', *Behavioral Research in Accounting*, Vol.5, pp.149-169.

Sikka, P (2004), 'Some questions about the governance of auditing firms', *International Journal of Disclosure and Governance*, Vol.1(2), pp.186-200.

Sikka, P (2001a), 'Regulation of Accountancy and the power of capital: Some observations', *Critical Perspectives on Accounting*, Vol.12(2), pp.199-211.

Sikka, P (2001b)'Transparency and accountability of the professional accountancy bodies: some observations on the Canning and O'Dwyer paper', *The European Accounting Review*, Vol.10(4), pp.751-761.

Sikka, P and H Willmott (1995), 'The power of 'Independence': Defending and Extending the jurisdiction of Accounting in the United Kingdom', *Accounting Organizations and Society*, Vol.20(6), pp.547–581.

Sikka, P, H C Willmott and T Lowe (1989), 'Guardians of knowledge and public interests: Evidence and issues of accountability in the UK accountancy professions', *Accounting, Auditing and Accountability Journal*, Vol.2(2), pp.47-71.

Sims, R R and J Brinkmann (2003), 'Enron Ethics (Or Culture Matters More than Codes)', *Journal of Business Ethics*, Vol.45(3), pp.243-256.

Singleton-Green, B (2002), 'Structure and Independence', *Accountancy*, March, p.23.

Smith, L M (2003), 'A fresh look at accounting ethics (or Dr Smith goes to Washington)' *Accounting Horizons*, March, Vol.17(1), pp.47-49.

Smith, T (1996), *Accounting for Growth: Stripping the camouflage from company accounts*, 2nd Edition, Century Books, London.

Staubus, G J (2005), 'Ethics failures in corporate financial reporting', *Journal of Business Ethics*, Vol.57(1), pp.5-15.

Staubus, G J (2004), 'On Brian P West's Professionalism and Accounting Rules', *Abacus*, Vol.40(2), pp.139-156.

Steiner, G A (1972), 'Social policies for business', *California Management Review*, Winter, pp.17-24.

Stewart, I C (1991), 'The ethics of disclosure in company financial reporting in the United Kingdom 1925-1970', *The Accounting Historians Journal*, Vol.18(1), pp.35-54.

Stumpf, S A, J P Doh and K D Clark (2002), 'Professional Services Firms in Transition: Challenges and opportunities for improving performance', *Organizational Dynamics*, Vol.31(3), pp.259-279.

Sutton M H (2002), 'Financial reporting at a crossroads', *Accounting Horizons*, Vol.16(4), pp.319-326.

Sutton, T G (1984), 'Lobbying of accounting standard-setting bodies in the U.K. and U.S.A.: A Downsian analysis', *Accounting, Organizations and Society*, Vol.9(1), pp.81-95.

Sweeney, B and B Pierce (2004), 'Management control in audit firms: a qualitative examination', *Accounting, Auditing & Accountability Journal*, Vol.17(5), pp.779-812.

Teoh, S H., I Welsh and T J Wong (1998), 'Earnings management and the underperformance of seasoned equity offers', *Journal of Financial Economics*, Vol.50(1), pp.63-99.

Teoh, S H, J Wong and G Rao (1998), 'Are accruals during initial public offerings opportunistic?', *Review of Accounting Studies*, Vol.3(1/2), pp.175-208.

Thorne, L (1998), 'The Role of Virtue in Auditors' Ethical Decision Making: An Integration of Cognitive-Developmental and Virtue-Ethics Perspectives', *Research on Accounting Ethics*, Vol.4, pp.291-308.

Toffler, B L (2003), *Final Accounting: Ambition, Greed, and the Fall of Arthur Andersen*, New York, Broadway Books.

Treadway Commission (1987), *The Report of the National Commission on Fraudulent Financial Reporting*, AICPA, New York.

Trevino, L (1986) 'Ethical decision making in organisations: A person-situation interactionist model', *Academy of Management Review*, 11(3), pp.601-617.

Tricker, B (1999), 'Editorial: Is company directorship a profession?', *Corporate Governance*, Vol.7(4), pp.309-310.

Tucker, L R, V Stathakopolous and C H Patti (1999), 'A Multidimensional Assessment of Ethical Codes: The Professional Business Association Perspective', *Journal of Business Ethics*, Vol.19(3), pp.287-300.

Unger, L (2001), *This year's proxy season: Sunlight shines on auditor independence and executive compensation*, June 25, available at: http://www.sec.gov/news/speech/spch502.htm.

Van Peursem, K A and A Hauriasi (1999), 'Auditors' reputation: an analysis of press coverage in New Zealand', *Accounting Forum*, March, Vol.23(1), pp.93-108.

Velayutham, S and H Perera (1993), 'The reflective accountant: towards a new model for professional development', *Accounting Education*, Vol.2(4), pp.287-301.

Velayutham, S and A Rahman (2000), 'Towards market differentiation in the accounting profession: The case of Australia and New Zealand', *Critical Perspectives on Accounting*, Vol.11(6), pp.691-711.

Wahlen, J (1994), 'The nature of information in commercial bank loan loss disclosures', *The Accounting Review*, Vol.69(3), July, pp.455-478.

Walker, S P (2004), 'The genesis of professional organisation in English accountancy', *Accounting, Organizations and Society*, Vol.29(2), pp.127-156.

Walker, S P (1996), 'The criminal upperworld and the emergence of a disciplinary code in the early chartered accountancy profession', *Accounting History*, Vol.1(2), pp.7-35.

Walker S P (1995), 'The Genesis of Professional Organization in Scotland: A Contextual Analysis', *Accounting, Organizations and Society*, Vol.20(4), pp.285-310.

Walker, S P (1988), *The Society of Accountants in Edinburgh, 1854-1914: A Study of Recruitment to a New Profession*, Garland Publishing.

Weil, J and S J Paltrow (2002), 'US Regulator found deficiencies in Peer Reviews', *The Wall Street Journal Europe*, 30 January.

West, B P (2003), *Professionalism and Accounting Rules*, Routledge, London.

West, B P (1996), 'The professionalisation of accounting: A review of recent historical research and its implications', *Accounting History*, Vol.1(1), pp.77-101.

Willett, C and M Page (1996), 'A survey of time budget pressure and irregular auditing practices among newly qualified UK chartered accountants', *British Accounting Review*, Vol.28(2), pp.101-120.

Williams, P F (2004), 'You reap what you sow: the ethical discourse of professional accounting', *Critical Perspectives on Accounting*, Vol.15(5/6), pp.995–1001.

Willis E (1983), *Medical Dominance*, George Allen and Unwin, Sydney.

Willmott, H (1986), 'Organizing the profession: A theoretical and historical examination of the development of the major accountancy bodies in the UK', *Accounting, Organizations and Society*, Vol.11(6), pp.555-580.

Willmott, H and P Sikka (1997), 'On the commercialization of accountancy thesis: A review essay', *Accounting, Organizations and Society*, Vol.22(8), pp.831-842.

Willmott, H, D Cooper and T Puxty (1993), 'Maintaining self-regulation: Making 'interests' coincide with discourses on the governance of the ICAEW', *Accounting, Auditing & Accountability Journal*, Vol.6(4), pp.68-93.

Wilson G P (2002), 'Don't throw out the reporting baby with the Enron bath water: critical considerations when reforming the reporting system', *Financial Reporting*, BDO Seidman, April.

Windsor, C A and N M Ashkanasy (1995), 'The effect of Client management bargaining power, moral reasoning development, and belief in a just world on auditor independence', *Accounting, Organizations and Society*, Vol.20(7/8), pp.701-720.

Wyatt, A R (2003), *Accounting Professionalism - They just don't get it!*, Plenary address - 2003 annual meeting of the American Accounting Association, available at http://aaahq.org/AM2003/WyattSpeech.pdf

Wyatt, A R (2004), 'Accounting Professionalism – They just don't get it!', *Accounting Horizons*, Vol.18(1), pp.45–53.

Young, J J (2005), 'Changing our questions: Reflections on the Corporate Scandals', *Accounting and the Public Interest*, Vol.5, pp.1-13.

Young, J J (1997), 'Defining Auditors' Responsibilities', *The Accounting Historians Journal*, Vol.24(2), pp.25-63.

Zeff, S A (2003a), 'Du Pont's early policy on the rotation of audit firms', *Journal of Accounting and Public Policy*, Vol.22(1), pp.1-18.

Zeff, S A (2003b), 'How the U.S. Accounting Profession Got Where It Is Today: Part I', *Accounting Horizons*, Vol.17(3), pp.189-205.

Zeff, S A (2003c), 'How the U.S. Accounting Profession Got Where It Is Today: Part II', *Accounting Horizons*, Vol.17(4), pp.267-286.

Zeff, S A (2002), 'Political Lobbying on proposed standards: A challenge to the IASB', *Accounting Horizons*, Vol.16(1), pp.43-54.

Zeff, S A (1986), 'Big Eight Firms and the Accounting Literature: The Falloff in advocacy Writing', *Journal of Accounting, Auditing and Finance*, Vol.1(2), pp.131-154.

Zeff, S A (1972), *Forging Accounting Principles in Five Countries: A History and Analysis of Trends*, Champaign IL: Stripes Publishing.